Emerging Prophet

"Following Kierkegaard, Roberts encourages and displays a healthy rhythm of critical distance and active engagement—funding both the critique of the idols of modernism, moralism, and Christendom, and the creative retrieval of a proper understanding of the revelation of God in Scripture and our imaginative, hermeneutical engagement with it."

—**CHRISTOPHER BEN SIMPSON**
author of *The Truth is the Way: Kierkegaard's Theologia Viatorum*

"To 'emergent' Christians experimenting with faith apart from the benefits of established Christianity, Roberts introduces Kierkegaard as an invaluable resource. To those of us who have wrestled with Kierkegaard, Roberts introduces a growing group of creative, faithful Christians who wrestle with radical discipleship. Whether they are scholars, students, or seekers, this book is for all who wonder and worry about the shape of Christian faith and church today."

—**JASON A. MAHN**
author of *Fortunate Fallibility: Kierkegaard and the Power of Sin*

"As emergent Christianity has gained more traction in the church, serious scholars have been paying attention and adding to the conversation. Rarely has a book been published in this vein about which I am as excited as I am about *Emerging Prophet*. To put the emerging church movement into conversation with Kierkegaard is, I think, a stroke of genius—it's a match made in heaven."

—**TONY JONES**
author of *The Church Is Flat: The Relational Ecclesiology of the Emerging Church Movement*

"In this compelling and well-written volume, Roberts brings the postmodern commitments of the emerging church into fruitful conversation with Kierkegaard. In so doing he makes a powerful case that emergence Christianity is generally consistent with Kierkegaard's vision of a Christian alternative to Christendom. This is one of the best books yet on the potential significance of the emerging church movement for the future of Christianity in the West."

—**JOHN R. FRANKE**
author of *Manifold Witness: The Plurality of Truth*

"At a time when the church is in the midst of transition, Roberts call out the passionate, ironic, scathing, beautiful voice of Kierkegaard to help us imagine faithful ecclesiological alternatives. It's a brilliant move—hopeful, generative, insightful, and instructive."

—**DEBBIE BLUE**
author of *From Stone to Living Word: Letting the Bible Live Again*

Emerging Prophet

Kierkegaard and the Postmodern People of God

KYLE A. ROBERTS

CASCADE Books • Eugene, Oregon

EMERGING PROPHET
Kierkegaard and the Postmodern People of God

Copyright © 2013 Kyle A. Roberts. All rights reserved. Except for brief quotations in critical publications or reviews, no part of this book may be reproduced in any manner without prior written permission from the publisher. Write: Permissions. Wipf and Stock Publishers, 199 W. 8th Ave., Suite 3, Eugene, OR 97401.

Cascade Books
An Imprint of Wipf and Stock Publishers
199 W. 8th Ave., Suite 3
Eugene, OR 97401

www.wipfandstock.com

ISBN 13: 978-1-61097-222-2

Cataloguing-in-Publication Data

Roberts, Kyle A.

    Emerging prophet : Kierkegaard and the postmodern people of God / Kyle A. Roberts

    xiv + 160 p. ; 23 cm. Includes bibliographical references.

    ISBN 13: 978-1-61097-222-2

    1. Kierkegaard, Søren, 1813–1855. 2. Postmodernism—Religious aspects—Christianity. 3. Emerging church movement. 4. Church renewal. I. Title.

B4377 R712 2013

Manufactured in the U.S.A.

For Sara, Ella, and Luke

. . . without risk, faith is an impossibility
—Kierkegaard

CONTENTS

Preface | ix
Acknowledgments | xi
List of Abbreviations | xiii

Introduction: Against Idolatry | 1

Chapter One
  Reclaiming Revelation | 13

Chapter Two
  Against Certainty | 35

Chapter Three
  Reclaiming Imagination | 64

Chapter Four
  Against Moralism | 85

Chapter Five
  Reclaiming Love | 106

Chapter Six
  Against Christendom | 126

Conclusion: Reclaiming the Restlessness of Faith | 146

Bibliography | 153

PREFACE

THIS BOOK REPRESENTS A long personal and theological journey. The connection between Kierkegaard and postmodern Christianity began, for me, during my college days at Wheaton, a flagship evangelical institution. As a philosophy and literature major in college, I found my faith deeply challenged during my senior year. There was no ill intent by any professor and my experience was by no means unusual. In my developmental process, as I encountered new ideas, I was pressing into a more complex faith. The complexities and questions had reached a tipping point. As I pressed into them further, due to a heavy dose of postmodern philosophy and critical analytic thought, I felt the foundation of my faith giving way. My bedrock of religious certainty, seemingly so stable up until then, was becoming precarious. On what—or on whom—was I standing? Ultimately, Kierkegaard's answer to my quandary was to assure me that what I was experiencing, in this time of questioning, was actually spiritual growth, not spiritual death. Kierkegaard helped me handle the disequilibrium and move into an embrace of a more ambiguous, more complex, and—I think—deeper faith. I have been reading and writing about Kierkegaard since.

At Wheaton, I also encountered emergent Christianity, in its embryonic form. Dr. Robert Webber was my first theology professor. He inspired many young evangelical low-church Protestants to explore liturgical traditions and to tap into the rich history of Christianity (mostly Anglicanism and Eastern Orthodoxy). A restlessness was afoot, as young Christians began experiencing and articulating their dissatisfaction with the seeker-sensitive, attractional, and pragmatic forms of evangelicalism. What Robert Webber called *The Younger Evangelicals* eventually matured into the emergent (or emerging) church.[1] For those who followed the Canterbury trail

---

1. Webber, *The Younger Evangelicals*.

(Anglicanism) or converted to Eastern Orthodoxy or Roman Catholicism, the postmodern ethos may—or may not—have been influential in their Christian journeys. They went *behind* modernity, rather than in front of it. But for other evangelicals and mainline Protestants working out what it means to be Christian by reimagining how to practice Christianity in a new, fresh way (and in a way that also honored and tapped into the richness of tradition), the emerging/emergent church became a movement to which they could attach and a conversation in which they could engage their questions. They were "emerging" in their quest for a more participatory and experiential, more mysterious, more theologically robust, and more socially aware faith. They were also emerging in a common quest for a faith that not only tolerated doubt, but viewed it as a friend of faith; they embraced a self-consciously humble epistemological framework. I discovered that faith (and church) could be deeper and more complex than *modernist* Christianity—in my case, traditional, conservative evangelicalism—had led me to believe.

My formal theological education culminated in a doctoral dissertation on Kierkegaard's religious philosophy and theology of Scripture. This book is not a rewrite of that dissertation, though I was able to salvage and put to use here some of the research I did in my dissertation. This book is my attempt to bring Kierkegaard's religious thought into dialogue with postmodern expressions of Christianity (i.e., the emergent or emerging church).

I am neither an emerging church leader nor a recognized emergent theologian. While I am not a regular, committed participant of a self-consciously emergent/emerging church, I have benefited greatly from observing (though not as often as I would like) the gatherings at Solomon's Porch in Minneapolis, a flagship emergent community under the leadership of Doug Pagitt. I am grateful to Doug and the community of Solomon's Porch for their welcoming spirit and for being a model of an alternative way to practice Christianity and to celebrate life in Christ together. I resonate with the ethos and objectives of emergent Christianity and am deeply empathetic with the theology driving much of the movement. I am convinced—more than ever—that Kierkegaard, the "emerging prophet," has a good deal to contribute to those who are attempting to live out an alternative vision of Christianity in our complex world.

ACKNOWLEDGMENTS

THIS BOOK WAS CONCEIVED as a coauthored project, with my friend and fellow Kierkegaard enthusiast, Myron Penner. A number of events happened along the way, including a career change for Myron (from the academy to full-time ministry, as an associate Anglican priest). As he entered his new role and other projects, I became the sole author. Without Myron's early creative vision, the project likely would not have gotten off the ground. I want to also thank my editor, Robin Parry, for his invaluable contribution to the idea of the book, and for his patience and encouragement throughout many twists, turns, and delays.

Kevin Vanhoozer, my doctoral advisor, was very influential on my early study of Kierkegaard's theology of Scripture and religious epistemology. His acute questions and penetrating theological wisdom continue to impact my thinking. I am also deeply grateful for Silas Morgan, my former student who has become my friend and colleague. Our long conversations about Kierkegaard, the church, and postmodern theology have benefited me deeply and influenced me in more ways than he knows. I also want to acknowledge the good work of several student research assistants. David Mowers offered his keen eye for clarity and deep theological insight at an early stage of the project. John Fournelle came along at a later stage with his editorial prowess, research skills, and existentialist heart. He helped me push over the hump. Former student Alex Blondeau also read a portion of the manuscript and offered valuable comments and questions. My friend and former colleague Darrin Sarisky provided helpful feedback on chapter 1.

Doug Pagitt and Tony Jones gave generously of their time, engaging me in a lengthy interview during the summer of 2011. That rich conversation helped crystalize much of my thinking in this book.

Some of my Kierkegaard research was undertaken at the Howard and Edna Hong Kierkegaard Library at St. Olaf College in Northfield; I appreciate the hospitality of Gordon Marino and Cynthia Lund. Their reputation for generosity and warmth is well deserved.

The artwork for the front cover comes from a painting given to me by my sister, Stephanie Roberts Addington. I am deeply thankful for her gift and am always amazed by her giftedness.

Finally, I want to thank the person who has sustained, encouraged, and helped me more than any other through these past several years: my wife, Sara. Her kindness, patience, and love have made the completion of this project not only possible, but a joy. She has been a tremendous source of support and inspiration.

ABBREVIATIONS

CA   *The Concept of Anxiety.* Edited and Translated by Howard V. Hong and Reidar Thomte. Princeton: Princeton University Press, 1980.

CD   *Christian Discourses* and *The Crisis and a Crisis in the Life of an Actress.* Edited and Translated by Howard V. Hong and Edna H. Hong. Princeton: Princeton University Press, 1997.

CUP *Concluding Unscientific Postscript to "Philosophical Fragments."* 2 vols. Edited and Translated by Howard V. Hong and Edna H. Hong. Princeton: Princeton University Press, 1992.

EO1 *Either/Or.* Volume I. Edited and Translated by Howard V. Hong and Edna H. Hong. Princeton: Princeton University Press, 1987.

EUD *Eighteen Upbuilding Discourses.* Edited and translated by Howard V. Hong and Edna H. Hong. Princeton: Princeton University Press, 1990.

FSE *For Self-Examination* (published with *Judge for Yourself!*). Edited and translated by Howard V. Hong and Edna H. Hong. Princeton: Princeton University Press, 1990.

FT   *Fear and Trembling.* Edited and translated by Howard V. Hong and Edna H. Hong. Princeton: Princeton University Press, 1983.

JFY *Judge for Yourself!* (published with *For Self-Examination*). Edited and translated by Howard V. Hong and Edna H. Hong. Princeton: Princeton University Press, 1990.

JP   *Journals and Papers.* Edited and translated by Howard V. Hong and Edna H. Hong. 6 vols. Princeton: Princeton University Press, 1967–78.

Pap.	*Søren Kierkegaard's Papirer* (Søren Kierkegaard's papers). 2nd enlarged edition by Niels Thulstrup, with index vols. 14–16 by Niels Jørgen Cappelørn. 16 vols. Copenhagen: Gyldendal, 1968–78.
PC	*Practice in Christianity*. Edited and translated by Howard V. Hong and Edna H. Hong. Princeton: Princeton University Press, 1991.
PF	*Philosophical Fragments*. Edited and translated by Howard V. Hong and Edna H. Hong. Princeton: Princeton University Press, 1985.
SLW	*Stages on Life's Way*. Edited and translated by Howard V. Hong and Edna H. Hong. Princeton: Princeton University Press, 1988.
SUD	*The Sickness Unto Death*. Edited and translated by Howard V. Hong and Edna H. Hong. Princeton: Princeton University Press, 1988.
TDIO	*Three Discourses on Imagined Occasions*. Edited and translated by Howard V. Hong and Edna H. Hong. Princeton: Princeton University Press, 1993.
TM	*The Moment and Late Writings*. Edited and translated by Howard V. Hong and Edna H. Hong. Princeton: Princeton University Press, 1985.
UDVS	*Upbuilding Discourses in Various Spirits*. Edited and translated by Howard V. Hong and Edna H. Hong. Princeton: Princeton University Press, 2005.
WA	*Without Authority*. Edited and translated by Howard V. Hong and Edna H. Hong. Princeton: Princeton University Press, 1997.
WL	*Works of Love*. Edited and translated by Howard V. Hong and Edna H. Hong. Princeton: Princeton University Press, 1995.

INTRODUCTION
Against Idolatry

Søren Kierkegaard is known as a philosopher (the "father of existentialism"), an eccentric genius, and a deeply religious thinker. His trenchant critique of Christendom—the institutionalized, established Christianity of nineteenth-century Denmark—ensured his fame as a religious discontent. Kierkegaard was increasingly disturbed by the nominalism and hypocrisy he perceived to be rampant in the Danish Lutheran state-church; his ire culminated in his infamous *Attack Upon Christendom*, in 1854–55. Kierkegaard spilled a good bit of ink these final years of his life attempting to point out what he perceived to be serious deficiencies in established Christianity. He sought after an existential and religious awakening; he longed for deeper *inwardness*, seriousness, and authenticity. He did not strategize a wide-scale structural reform or attempt a new reformation. He simply wanted to awaken a new existential and religious honesty—an "admission" that the Christianity expressed in Denmark was an inadequate representation of the New Testament. Along with seeking honesty, he worked toward the "inward deepening" of his readers. His project was aimed at the edification of the *single individual*—his beloved reader. Through his writing, he hoped to instill a desire for a more authentic religious experience in any who would take up his challenge. He articulated an understanding of Christianity that was motivated by love, shaped by the Spirit, and impelled toward its centripetal reality—Jesus Christ, the God-man, whom Kierkegaard called the "absolute paradox." For Kierkegaard, true, inward, passionate Christianity means following Christ, which results in "collisions" with the world. New Testament faith is a "restless thing."[1]

1. *FSE*, 18.

Emerging Prophet

Kierkegaard was a kind of prophet, but a prophet whose incisive voice transcends his time. Much of the situation of his day is still reflected in the "Western" world, in particular U.S. Anglo-Christianity. In many ways, some of the problems of modernity (several of which Kierkegaard was very quick to recognize) are still with us. This may be particularly true in deeply *modernist* forms of Christianity today, in both its liberal and conservative evangelical forms. His prophetic voice is relevant to and should be welcomed by postmodern Christians in our present age, who sense an opportunity to revitalize our theology and practice of Christianity.

In this respect, Kierkegaard shares some important elements in common with *emergent Christianity*, that postmodern-oriented renewal movement taking place within (and beyond) both evangelicalism and mainline Protestantism.[2] Kierkegaard manifests the type of prophetic consciousness described by Walter Brueggemann: "The task of prophetic ministry is to nurture, nourish, and evoke a consciousness and perception alternative to the consciousness and perception of the dominant culture around us."[3] Modern Christianity, in both its conservative and liberal forms, has distorted what Kierkegaard called the *essentially Christian* by accepting modernism's assumptions regarding the supreme authority of human reason, by elevating morality to the highest plane of human existence, by subsuming genuine difference under the ideal of universality, and by trusting its institutions (cultural, religious, social, etc.) over the passionate subjectivity of the human person.[4] Modernism perpetuates cognitive, moral, doctrinal, ethnocentric, and institutional idolatry and ultimately leads to a failure to love one's neighbor as oneself. Kierkegaard's "proto-postmodernist" prophetic voice attempted a deconstruction of the idols and ideologies of modernity.[5] This is why I believe Kierkegaard offers

---

2. Phyllis Tickle, in *Emergence Christianity*, employs this term to capture the broader cultural movement in which Christianity finds itself, linking the movement historically to the Pentecostal revivals at the turn of the twentieth century. I primarily use the term *emergent* throughout the book to designate that stream of Emergence Christianity, or the "emerging church," that is self-consciously empathetic with elements of postmodernity and that attempts to renew or move beyond traditional, modernist forms of Christianity. On the difference, see also Brewin's *Signs of Emergence*, 35.

3. Brueggemann, *Prophetic Imagination*, 13.

4. I define Kierkegaard's understanding of the *essentially Christian* in chapter 1.

5. Bruce Benson, in *Graven Ideologies*, notes the similarities between idols and ideologies. Idols "are images we create . . . and invariably these images are reflections of ourselves" (22). An ideology, Benson explains, is "a nothing that passes itself off as something and seduces one into belief" (25). Both differ from *icons*, which, while they

Introduction

a timely and prophetic voice for postmodern Christians, those who are seeking a fresh, deeply authentic way to practice the Christian faith in our complex, challenging world. Kierkegaard is a thought-guide—a sage—for Christians who empathize with postmodern sensibilities and dispositions toward life and faith.[6] The philosophical and theological ramifications of Kierkegaard's thought will be unpacked throughout the rest of the book, but as an initial characterization, Kierkegaard's account of New Testament Christianity involves a critique of both liberalism *and* fundamentalism (i.e., conservative evangelicalism) as modernist distortions.[7]

This journey is fraught with dangers. As anyone familiar with Kierkegaard will acknowledge, he cannot easily be taken up in the service of any "project." And when he is, with all the fear and trembling one can muster, one must be mindful that his thoughts wound as much as they heal. But as we know with any good prophetic literature, the wounding *is* the healing. Kierkegaard has much to say to forms and movements of Christianity that want to live out their faith authentically, with an openness to truth, with a keen eye to actuality (or, the practical and concrete), with a heart for the plight of humanity and of existence, with a deep love for the Scriptures, with a respect for truth, and with an abiding fascination and reverence for the mystery of Christ. In fact, there is so much resonance across Kierkegaard's thought (variegated and complex as it is) and postmodern expressions of Christianity that I am surprised at how little the connection has been reflected on. Many scholars have undertaken to explore Kierkegaard's thought in relation to postmodern philosophy and theology generally. The influence of Kierkegaard on John Caputo, a philosopher and theologian associated with the postmodern ethos within Christian thought, is a strong

---

are images, reflect and mediate *substance*.

6. For a description and analysis of postmodernity generally, see Best and Kellner, *The Postmodern Turn*. For a *theological* description and analysis of the "postmodern turn," see Myron Penner's introductory essay in Penner, *Christianity and the Postmodern Turn*, 13–36.

7. I am using "fundamentalism" here in a broad sense, *not* to designate the anti-modernist subculture out of which evangelicalism emerged as a distinct response to modernism. Rather, it designates, more broadly, theologically and socially conservative evangelicalism today: those who not only emphatically affirm the doctrinal "fundamentals" determined to be central to Christianity, but who adhere to a foundationalist epistemology (this will be explained in chapter 2) and a biblicist mentality that succumbs to bibliolatry. Throughout the book, I mostly use "conservative evangelical" as a synonym for fundamentalism, and in distinction from post-conservative, moderate, progressive, or postmodern evangelical.

3

example.[8] Similarly, the work of philosopher Merold Wesphal stands out. But not much has been done to relate Kierkegaard's thought directly to emergent Christianity. That is the purpose of this book: to directly engage the religious thought of Kierkegaard with thinkers associated with or influential on emergent Christianity. This book is neither a heavily technical book on Kierkegaard's philosophy nor a detailed analysis of postmodern thought, but an engagement of Kierkegaard's prophetic religious philosophy with emergent Christianity and emergent theology. I also trust the book will serve as both a helpful introduction to Kierkegaard's understanding of Christianity and a synopsis of emergent theology.

This book is not an empirical study of the movement and its churches, but a dialogical engagement with the published theological reflections of its leaders and other thinkers who have influenced the movement. The future of emergent Christianity does not depend on the existence and persistence of discrete communities that explicitly define themselves as postmodern, emergent, emerging, or some other related category. Such exclusions can run against the embrace and promotion of the very diversity the postmodern turn is said to value. In my opinion, emergent Christianity will continue to experience so many shifts and variations of expression in the coming years that it will become nearly impossible (and will be counterproductive, besides) to divvy up the labels and demarcate one from the other. The fluidity suggested by the terms *emerging* and *emergent* suggest that final divisions and definitive labels should be avoided. Christians—and ensembles or collectives of Christians who accept, howsoever and critically and cautiously, the postmodern turn (or whatever "ism" we may now be shifting to)—will be located in all sorts of church contexts, whether in traditionally "institutional" Christian churches, in emergent collectives, in house churches, and some in none at all.

I should acknowledge that, with increasing fervor, scholars and other cultural observers are predicting (or even pronouncing) the looming death of postmodernism. However, until we know what "ism" we are now in (or rather, until scholars come to some consensus), we still must contend with the actual phenomena that persist in our culture and the intellectual milieu we have come to call the "postmodern turn." Furthermore, I am of the opinion that postmodernism persists. Certainly, many of the prominent features of postmodernity persist in Western societies: tolerance of ambiguity, embrace of plurality, recognition of the indeterminacy (or at

---

8. See Caputo, *Radical Hermeneutics*, and *How to Read Kierkegaard*.

least incompleteness) of meaning, respect for individuality, suspicion of authority ("metanarratives"), to cite just a few examples. In any case, I am more interested in the shared phenomena, concerns, and values of emergent Christianity, a movement that—contrary to many of its conservative critics—remains a formidable presence on the contemporary religious landscape.[9]

WHAT IS EMERGENT CHRISTIANITY?

Tony Jones, formerly director of Emergent Village and currently an influential emergent theologian, offers a helpful summary of definitions of emergent/emerging in his recent book, *The Church Is Flat*. There, Jones points to the *Encyclopedia of Religion in America*, which states, "The emerging church movement is a loosely aligned conversation among Christians who seek to reimagine the priorities, values and theology expressed by the local church as it seeks to live out its faith in postmodern society. It is an attempt to replot Christian faith on a new cultural and intellectual terrain."[10] In his book, Jones offers a thicker theological description of the movement by attending to the virtues, practices, and theological emphases that unite practitioners and participants in the movement.

Katharine Sarah Moody, writing on the emerging church (often called "fresh expressions") in the United Kingdom, suggests it should be thought of less in terms of static identity and more in terms of "milieu."[11] A milieu signifies cohesion of shared concerns, values, discourses, friendships, and practices, without eliminating differences between subgroups and individuals in the set. Emergent Christianity is not exclusive to any major Christian tradition (e.g., Protestantism or Roman Catholicism) or to a denomination (e.g., Presbyterian or Methodist). There is no creed that defines it and no statement of faith that circumscribes it. In the past, it has been described as primarily a conversation, or dialogue; however, it has become clear that the emergent movement is more than a conversation, academic or otherwise.[12] Those involved with and invested in emergent

---

9. For elaboration and defense of this point, see Tickle, *The Great Emergence*; Jones, *The Church Is Flat*; and Bass, *Christianity After Religion*.

10. Jones, *Church Is Flat*, 5; Bird, "Emerging Church Movement," 682.

11. Moody, "I Hate Your Church." Moody borrowed the term *milieu* from Gordon Lynch's assessment of progressive spirituality in *New Spirituality*, 12.

12. In an interview I conducted with Tony Jones and Doug Pagitt (2011), Jones noted

Christianity recognize that *something is afoot*. It is comprised of individuals and communities who are creatively seeking fresh, vibrant, authentic forms of Christian faith and church that resonate with postmodern sensibilities concerning the nature of (and access to) truth; the value of dialogue; the nature of religious authority and sacred texts; skepticism of received interpretations and established (authoritarian) doctrines; preference for organic, egalitarian structures; openness to otherness and embrace of plurality; and an approach to the Christian life as a *quest*, or journey, rather than a fixed identity with a closed destination.

To look ahead for a moment, here is one key place where Kierkegaard and emergent Christianity connect. Kierkegaard provides a possible way through the maze of an undefined, hopeful, but often confused postmodern faith. How do we know what is true? How do we talk about truth at all? What is the nature of revelation? What role does the Bible play in all this? How should we read it? *Why* should we read it? What is the relation between theology and truth? How should we communicate our faith in this post-Christian, pluralist world? How can the Christian church be post-Constantinian and nontriumphalist (i.e., humble) without losing long-standing, central convictions (i.e., "Jesus is Lord")? What is genuine faith? What does it mean to love the "other"? What does the imitation of Christ involve? In what should the ethical and political life consist? As a guide in the quest for an existentially authentic faith, Kierkegaard helps us think through possible answers to these questions. Sometimes he is more than a guide, because he can speak downright prophetically.

Emergent Christianity, recognizing the both the theological inadequacies and the loosening grip of modernity, has attempted to find a place beyond between modernist liberal Protestantism and modernist conservative evangelicalism. They have attempted to construct a different way of conceiving of Christianity and the church. My sense, both in my experiential observations and in reading the literature, is that, in many ways, the concerns that give rise to emergent Christianity parallel Kierkegaard's critique of Christendom in his own context. Tim Keel, pastor of Jacob's Well (Kansas City), illustrates here what I mean:

---

that emergent Christianity's mistake, in the early days, was to emphasize the "conversation" motif rather than seek to articulate and assert positive, theological themes and values. He did not mean by this a creed or confession of faith, but a kind of collective, constructive theological task that did not shy away from asserting theological beliefs.

Introduction

I believe the emerging church phenomenon is but one small example of an alternative attempt to engage reality. The emerging church strives to re-fathom who God is, what the gospel is, how we access and read Scripture, what it means to be human, and how we generate a common life in the midst of creation in response to these realities. We are seeking freedom from captivity to a mindset that does not seem true to life as we experience it nor capable of incorporating our emerging understandings of reality.[13]

In subsequent chapters, we will discover that Kierkegaard can help us deconstruct the idols that have been passed down from our modernist forebears and that continue to obstruct our worship. Kierkegaard helps us recover a robust, christocentric theology of revelation, a view of truth as personal engagement ("subjectivity"), a positive view of the imagination in biblical interpretation and theology, the church's vocation to be witnesses to Christ through *works of love*, and the intimate, vulnerable (kenotic) nature of Christian community. Kierkegaard can inspire us—in particular those in concert with the movement called emergent Christianity—to be, as Keel suggests, an "alternative attempt to engage reality" by deconstructing the idols and idolatries of modernism. In short, postmodern Christians are dissatisfied with the modernist distortion of what Kierkegaard called the essentially Christian.

A TINY BIT ABOUT KIERKEGAARD

There is not space here for a biography of Kierkegaard or an extensive introduction to his corpus.[14] However, it is imperative to point out that, as a Danish Lutheran, he was *emphatically* a religious and Christian author. Christianity deeply influenced his writings, from first to last. Kierkegaard's formation as a Christian took place at the intersection of state-church Lutheranism and Moravian pietism. The influence of Kierkegaard's pietistic father on the young Kierkegaard's religious sensibilities is well documented. While he remained faithfully within the Danish state church, he also exposed the family to a local Moravian community. Kierkegaard attended these meetings with his father as a child; the religiosity he observed

---

13. Keel, "Leading from the Margins," 230.

14. For readers interested in his biography, see Lowrie, *A Short Life of Kierkegaard*, and Garff, *Søren Kierkegaard*. For readers looking for an introduction to his works and thought, see Evans, *Kierkegaard: An Introduction*; Ferreira, *Kierkegaard*; Barrett, *Kierkegaard*; and Caputo, *How to Read Kierkegaard*.

7

through this pietist influence left a profound and lasting impression on him.¹⁵ This influence is most consistently evident in Kierkegaard's focus on the individual's relationship to God, the primacy of a living, personal relation to Christ over correctness or precision of doctrinal knowledge, and the significant role of the Bible (especially the New Testament) in mediating relational knowledge of God.¹⁶

Occasionally evangelicals will ask me whether Kierkegaard was really a Christian. To those familiar with his biography and his writings, the question is ironic (though the answer is complicated). Kierkegaard was clearly a Christian, in that he was a member of the Danish Lutheran church, was deeply influenced by his father's deep (and stern) piety, possessed profoundly religious sensibilities, and was theologically orthodox. Kierkegaard's life project—at least as he came to understand it—was to "reintroduce New Testament Christianity into Christendom."¹⁷ He was deeply committed to the primacy of the person of Christ (the "God-man") and interpreted his own life in large part through categories available in Christian theology. He based much of his thinking on the Bible, writing numerous "religious discourses" (philosophical and theological reflections on biblical texts) alongside his more philosophical works. The question of whether Kierkegaard was a Christian is ironic; he might want to turn the question around: Are *you* a Christian? Am I? How can we be sure? The complicated nature of the question is due to the fact that Kierkegaard often refused to *claim* to be a Christian. As we will see, for Kierkegaard, no one *is* a Christian; we are always *becoming* Christian. Kierkegaard's concern was to awaken people in Denmark from the illusion that they were Christians as a matter of course (simply by being Danish or by being members of the state church). Kierkegaard believed that the New Testament's understanding of Christianity is akin to a journey, or a quest (a "striving"); Christianity

---

15. Though Kierkegaard sparingly referenced the classical pietists in his works, his appreciation for them is evident in a late (1850) journal entry: "Yes, indeed, pietism (properly understood, not simply in the sense of abstaining from dancing and such externals, no, in the sense of witnessing for the truth and suffering for it, together with the understanding that suffering in this world belongs to being a Christian, and that a shrewd and secular conformity with this world is unchristian)—yes, indeed, pietism is the one and only consequence of Christianity." *Journals and Papers* (hereafter cited as *JP*), vol. 3, entry 524.

16. See also Barnett, *Kierkegaard, Pietism and Holiness*.

17. *JP* 4, 6271.

means following Christ on a path of suffering toward spiritual authenticity, or *inwardness*.[18]

A NOTE ABOUT HIS AUTHORSHIP

It is customary (and obligatory) in any book dealing with Kierkegaard to state how one approaches his complex authorship. Kierkegaard famously used an imaginative stable of pseudonymns, fictional names he ascribed as "authors" of a number of his books. His non-pseudonymous texts are known as his *signed* works—unambiguously written by Kierkegaard as Kierkegaard. The interpretive question is, how or to what extent should the pseudonymous texts be read differently from the signed works? Kierkegaard requested in an appendix to *Concluding Unscientific Postscript*, one of his pseudonymous works, that his readers—in particular, those scholars who would write about him—ascribe the pseudonymous works to the pseudonym, and not to Kierkegaard.[19] And yet, Kierkegaard took ultimate credit for the entire corpus, even his pseudonymous works, as their "editor."[20] So what do we do?

Hermeneutical theorists distinguish between the "empirical" author and the "implied" author of texts. For the purposes of interpretation (and *meaning*), readers are most interested in the implied author—the narrator embedded in or implied by the text. The empirical (historical) author is

---

18. Christopher Ben Simpson, in *The Truth Is the Way*, suggests the *theologia viatorum* to be a defining metaphor for Kierkegaard's authorship; it is, Simpson explains, "a wayfarer's theology, a theology for one on the way, for a traveller" (1). Kierkegaard understood the Christian life to be a journey in which the kingdom is the goal and Jesus Christ is the guide, "the pattern for us" (7).

19. At the end of *Concluding Unscientific Postscript*, Kierkegaard asked—rather, *pleaded*—that his readers and interpreters refer to the respective pseudonymous authors when referencing pseudonymous texts. He wrote, "Thus in the pseudonymous books there is not a single word by me" (*CUP*, 626). He chose to ascribe his works to pseudonyms because he wanted to present various points of view without his own identity as author getting in the way. As he states, "A pseudonym is excellent for accentuating a point, a stance, a position. He is a poetic person. Therefore, it is not as if I personally said: This is what I am fighting for . . ." (*JP* 6, 6421).

20. ". . . I am still part of it as editor and will, in fact, take the responsibility, and everything will be understood as if I myself said it. Consequently there is nevertheless a very essential step forward, both in getting it said and in the actual attribution to me. The plus here is really this: that while the one who is speaking is indeed no one, a pseudonym, the editor is an actual person and one who acknowledges that he is judged by what this pseudonym is saying" (*JP* 6, 6578).

often, for interpretive purposes, irrelevant (and often quite literally dead). In this book, I am interested in the implied author—or more specifically, the *matter* and meaning of these texts. Sometimes Kierkegaard's empirical life (his biography) is helpful for interpretation and sometimes the function of a particular pseudonym is hermeneutically useful. But by and large, the text itself (and the implied author) is what matters.[21] While I will occasionally refer to a pseudonym, in deference to Kierkegaard's stated wish, I will use "Kierkegaard" generally to denote the implied author of his vast corpus of work (remember that Kierkegaard considered himself the "general editor" of the entire authorship). Throughout this book, I am interested in the religious significance of Kierkegaard's thought and engaging it with emergent Christianity.

A PREVIEW OF THIS BOOK

In chapter 1, I argue that Kierkegaard's prophetic, alternative consciousness is impelled by his conviction that God speaks into the human experience; there is such a thing as *divine revelation*. For Kierkegaard, this revelation occurs most centrally in the person of Jesus Christ. In chapter 2, I examine the personal and transformational nature of Kierkegaard's prophetic declaration that *truth is subjectivity*. Christian truth is *subjectively* (not objectively) oriented and requires personal, passionate, and authentic appropriation. This resonates with the emergent understanding that Christianity is not primarily a conceptual belief system, the existential significance of which depends upon objective understanding of doctrine. In chapter 3, I develop the idea that the journey, or quest, that marks the essentially Christian calls for an active use of the religious and hermeneutical imagination, both for individuals and for communities. To worship, to theologize, and to interpret the authoritative source of the Bible in today's context (postmodernity) requires that the religious imagination be brought back from the recesses to which modernity had relegated it. A dynamic view of Scripture, an understanding of its relational authority, and a retrieval of a positive role for the imagination explains and justifies contextual differences regarding how the Bible is interpreted and applied.

---

21. Kierkegaard did not want the transformative force of his texts to be undermined by the tendency of readers to turn their attention to the matter of the historical author's life. In other words, the pseudonyms were meant to detract from the *person* Kierkegaard so as to underscore the *matter* of the texts.

Introduction

In chapter 4, I explore Kierkegaard's understanding of sin, atonement, and the kind of idolatry he was against: the idolatry of placing human moral agency (moralism) over the God-relationship. Christianity is not defined by moralism, but by an existential orientation to its center in Jesus Christ, which results in a healthy relation of the self to God, the self to itself, and the self to others. While emergent thinkers resonate with a gracious and love-centered view of the atonement, I explore the idea that Kierkegaard's view of sin might be a helpful supplement to a potential weakness in emergent theology. In chapter 5, I show that, for Kierkegaard, an understanding of the ethical life requires a proper ordering of the ethical sphere to the religious; the religious transcends and orders the ethical. Finally, in chapter 6, I pursue Kierkegaard's understanding of the primacy of love in the Christian life and his conviction that kenotic *works of love* and suffering enable authentic witness to the essentially Christian. Kierkegaard critiques the idols and idolatries of power on the basis of the *imago Dei* and by advocating Christ as the "pattern." A return to a robust faith in and imitation of Christ results in an authentic, crucified church as Christians allow the power of Christ to deconstruct idols and open up ways of serving and loving the world. Also in chapter 6, I follow those insights by articulating an understanding of the identity and vocation of the church in our postmodern context, through engagement with Kierkegaard and emergent thinkers.

Throughout this book, I attempt to articulate a properly theological (Christ-centered) understanding of divine revelation and Scripture, a humble but passionate epistemology, an imaginative hermeneutic, a robust biblical theology of sin and atonement, an ethic of witness (based on the priority of love), and an ecclesiology (doctrine of the church) that counters the institutional excesses of Christendom with a humble, cruciform witness to the living Christ. I will attempt to articulate the Christian journey as a quest for an authentic faith, embodied by the postmodern people of God in works of love.

Chapter One

RECLAIMING REVELATION

"The Holy Scriptures are the highway signs, Christ is the way."[1]

Kierkegaard's critique of nineteenth-century Danish Christianity's capitulation to modernist epistemology revolved, in large part, around its theologically inadequate understanding of the Bible and of divine revelation. His critical analysis of nineteenth-century Christianity and his dynamic view of the nature of Scripture serve as a resource for contemporary theology and postmodern Christians in articulating a compelling doctrine of Scripture today. Much of the Christian church seems wedged between two boulders: On the one side, modernity's capitulation to Western rationality (in both its liberal and conservative forms) with its "inflated sense of epistemic certainty";[2] on the other, the temptation now present in some expressions of postmodernism to succumb to relativity and hermeneutical nihilism, thereby relinquishing any epistemic ground for religious practice and theological belief. In the face of both tendencies, Kierkegaard has this to say: God still speaks. Are you listening?

A temptation within modernist forms of evangelical Christianity is to fall prey to *bibliolatry*, a form of cognitive idolatry, in which the words on the page (the locutions, in speech-act theory) of the Bible become the ultimate

---

1. *JP* 1, 208.
2. Sparks, *God's Word in Human Words*, 231.

authority for the Christian life, usurping God. As N. T. Wright points out, the Bible's authority derives from the authority of God, not the other way around; it is a *derivative authority*.[3] Furthermore, in the Gospel of John, we find that a relationship with *Jesus*, not the Scriptures, is the means to salvation and relationship with God (John 5:39–40). In Kierkegaard's view, the Bible primarily facilitates a relationship with Jesus; it is an occasion for confrontation with Christ. Kierkegaard's prophetic call prompts the church to renew its understanding of Scripture as the living, breathing Word of God. This renewal requires at least three components: (1) a realization that, ultimately, revelation is about the person of Christ and is the relational disclosure of the living God; (2) an acknowledgment that the Bible's authority derives from the authority of God; and (3) emphasis on one's subjective relation to revelation. Only by subjective *appropriation* of revelation does it function for its intended purpose of facilitating authentic Christian existence. For Kierkegaard, the appropriation of the truth of revelation differs from mere application. Appropriation means *making the truth your own*; it is the personal assimilation of truth such that it transforms one's self.[4]

A few preliminary observations must be noted: this means that Scripture should not become an object to master or an instrument of power and control, used to suppress or oppress others. Nor should it be treated solely as an "objective" text, useful for developing cognitive, academic theologies (or doctrine for doctrine's sake). This chapter commends Kierkegaard's view of revelation and biblical authority as a way beyond the impasse caused by, on the one hand, modernity's capitulation to human reason (in both its liberal and fundamentalist forms) and, on the other hand, the temptation present in postmodernism to succumb to epistemic relativity or hermeneutic nihilism.[5] Kierkegaard's Scripture principle grounds the church in authoritative revelation without sacrificing the dynamic, passionate, and personal nature of the essentially Christian.

---

3. Wright, "How Can the Bible Be Authoritative?"

4. Jolita Pons, in *Stealing a Gift*, offers a succinct definition of Kierkegaard's understanding of appropriation: "Appropriation means to make truth your own (proper to you), to internalize it, to convert it into a reality within yourself" (46).

5. For an elaboration of epistemic relativity and hermeneutic nihilism, respectively, see chapters 2 and 3 in this book.

Emerging Prophet

KIERKEGAARD AND THE ESSENTIALLY CHRISTIAN

For Kierkegaard, the essence of authentic Christian faith is captured in his phrase "the essentially Christian." As Sylvia Walsh explains, "the essentially Christian is the rigor of existentially actualizing the qualifications of Christian existence."[6] The ideologies of modernity (*modernism*) neglected existential passion, or personal engagement with truth and the "actualizing" of knowledge. They did not recognize that genuine engagement with truth requires putting it into practice—what Kierkegaard called "reduplication."[7] In the hands of modernists, the substance of Christian faith was replaced by the idolatry (and ideologies) of rationalism, materialism, nationalism, and moralism. As a prophet of idol-deconstruction, Kierkegaard described his task as articulating the essentially Christian.[8]

The essentially Christian, then, is Christian faith lived with authenticity and rigor, stripped of the cumbersome layers of philosophical speculation, doctrinal accretions, and institutional dead weight. The essentially Christian is *action*, but a particular kind of action. In *Works of Love,* Kierkegaard says, "But the essentially Christian, which is not related to knowing but to acting, has the singular characteristic of answering and by means of the answer imprisoning everyone in the task."[9] To understand the essentially Christian is to grasp that Christianity calls us to action—ultimately, to the practice of self-denial and love, which involves faith, because it requires going "through offense."[10] It also requires the realization that Christianity is a *quest,* or—to use Kierkegaard's own term—a "striving."

---

6. Walsh, *Living Christianly,* 7. Here Walsh references *JP* 1, 518.

7. As Kierkegaard noted, "When Christianity (precisely because it is not a doctrine) does not reduplicate itself in the one who presents it, he does not present Christianity; for Christianity is an existential-communication and can only be presented—by existing. Basically, to exist therein [*at existere deri*], to express it in one's existence, etc.—this is what it means to reduplicate" (*JP* 1, 484). See also Walsh, *Living Christianly,* 10.

8. "My activity with regard to the essentially Christian. It is to nail down the Christian qualifications in such a way that no doubt, no reflection, shall be able to get hold of them. It is like locking the door and throwing away the key; thus the Christian qualifications are made inaccessible to reflection. Only the choice remains: will you believe or will you not believe, but the chatter of reflection cannot get hold of it" (*JP* 1, 522). Kierkegaard was not against all doubt: only the kinds of doubts that result from "reflection," or an "objective" (rational/philosophical) approach to Christian faith.

9. *WL,* 96.

10. *WL,* 29, 59, 114.

Reclaiming Revelation

The essentially Christian is not doctrine, speculation, or intellectual reflection, each of which avoids the strenuousness of action.[11]

THE NECESSITY OF DIVINE REVELATION FOR AUTHENTIC (CHRISTIAN) EXISTENCE

Kierkegaard shared little of his contemporaries' unbridled enthusiasm for the Enlightenment, of which Immanuel Kant's *sapere aude* ("Dare to know!") became the rallying cry. Objectivity and the explanatory power of rationality had been hailed as the harbinger of scientific progress and technological advancement; increasingly, this optimism transferred to the religious sphere as well. In the nineteenth century, during the precarious height of modernity, enthusiasm for the progresses of the Enlightenment was palpable and yet, in certain quarters (e.g., both orthodox and pietistic forms of Christianity and Romantic streams of philosophy) it was already waning. In the nineteenth century, some philosophers and theologians began to critique this (modernist) triumphalism, optimism, and faith in the power of human rationality. The twentieth-century existentialist movement, which hails Kierkegaard as a forerunner, was in large part a response to the failed optimism of modernity regarding historical progress on the basis of supposedly objective rationality. In the rush to proclaim the advent of universal reason, thinkers deluded by the power of human reason had both overestimated and underestimated the capabilities of finite, human people in the acquisition and application of knowledge. They overestimated the capacity of human reason to master the world via attainment of universal and comprehensive knowledge; and they underestimated the influence of the human passions ("subjectivity") and the negative factor of human sin in the quest for truth and mastery over the world (and each other). Kierkegaard rejected the common assumption that the maximization of the potentials of human rationality was sufficient for cultural progress and—more importantly—for individual human fulfillment (or becoming a *self*). For Kierkegaard, the age of reason had forgotten the necessity of divine revelation.

Nonetheless, the tension between faith and reason, so acutely recognized since the beginnings of Greek philosophy and throughout Christian history, had been seemingly resolved, as reason and science took center stage. In intellectual arenas, philosophers had begun to marginalize the

---

11. Walsh, *Kierkegaard: Thinking Christianly*, 32–34.

role of divine revelation—or exclude it altogether—in interpreting reality. From the other side of the divide, orthodox theologians and church leaders began to emphasize the objectivity of theology, the power of propositional doctrine, and the authority of the Bible in an effort to combat rising secularism. In effect, they attempted to secure the Bible as an apologetic support for Christian faith and turned it into a sourcebook for the compilation of objective doctrines. Kierkegaard walked into the middle of this struggle and articulated and modeled a Christ-centric view of revelation and of the Bible that underscored its dynamic, transformational power, its existential significance, and the necessity of personal, subjective appropriation.

In a journal entry, Kierkegaard gave us a glimpse into his intention to use "reflection," or dialectical thought, as a counterpoint to Hegelian reflection, in order to reestablish Scripture's authority:

> The divine authority of the Bible and everything related to it has been abolished; it looks as if one final unit of reflection is expected to finish the whole thing. But look, reflection is on the way to do a counterservice, to reset the coil springs in the essentially Christian so that it can stand its ground—against reflection.[12]

Kierkegaard's response to what he perceived to be the inadequacies of modernity involved a restoration of a proper, theological place for divine revelation. He advocated passionate, subjective involvement in knowledge, challenging the notion that rationality is a neutral tool and that objectivity is the optimal approach to religious knowledge. Kierkegaard was a proto-postmodernist, in that he anticipated the postmodernist critique of modernity's tendency to valorize a particular construal of rationality as universal and (merely) objective. What counts as knowledge, or as truth, is contingent on situation, perspective, and experience—in short, on context. Reason cannot provide unmediated access to reality (certainly not when the reality is the religious), nor can it be the final say in legitimating knowledge claims. Nonetheless, Kierkegaard's emphasis on human subjectivity was not a concession to absolute relativism, but a reminder that the human situation necessitates active, personal (the *whole* person), and relational engagement in the pursuit of religious knowledge and divine truth. The most significant existential and religious truths (e.g., the issue of eternal salvation) lie outside the access of mere rationality and scientific method. The reassertion of the role of divine revelation was an answer to the slippage of

---

12. *JP* 3, 3704.

modernity into the narcissism and naiveté of objectivity. For Kierkegaard, the appropriation of revelation, or *suprarational*, relational, and divinely given truth, was required for personal and spiritual development.[13]

The "Theological Self": Kierkegaard on Personal and Spiritual Development

For Kierkegaard, every person's task is to become a *self*; it is "eternity's claim upon him."[14] The complexity of human beings means that this task is a struggle. A person develops as a self over time in an arduous process of relational becoming. The self emerges as a dialectical synthesis of the eternal and the temporal, of freedom and necessity: "it is composed of infinitude and finitude."[15] The self must strive to become a unified self by a dialectic process of engaging the eternal and the temporal; this begins with a turn inward. This inward turn, to the eternal (infinite) mode of the human self, invites the self's development through the spheres, or stages, of existence: the aesthetic, the ethical, and what he calls religiousness A and B.[16] Inhabitation of the various spheres of existence reflects the quest of a self in his or her task of relating to God. To become a self is to learn (experientially) how to relate "absolutely to the absolute telos and relatively to the relative."[17] It is to have one's idolatries exposed and to accept one's position as a sinner before God. But the achievement of unity in a person, as a complete self, requires a right relation of the self to God and a concrete grounding in one's recognition of sin (and despair) and one's need for God. As Kierkegaard's pseudonymous author Anti-Climacus put it: "The self is

---

13. Emmanuel, *Kierkegaard and the Concept of Revelation*, 52–55.

14. *SUD*, 21

15. *SUD*, 29.

16. The more commonly recognized translation "stages," as in *Stages on Life's Way*, has a better counterpart in the rendering "spheres" of existence, or existence-spheres. As James Collins points out, this latter translation captures Kierkegaard's view that the spheres (stages) of existence are not necessarily chronologically ordered steps, as on a ladder, but are "modes of life," which are reached by a decisive leap by the individual. One does not necessarily have to begin with the aesthetic stage, move to the ethical, and then to the religious; rather, one can make the "leap" from the aesthetic to the religious, or bypass the aesthetic altogether. See Collins, *Mind of Kierkegaard*, 42–50.

17. *CUP*, 431–32.

the conscious synthesis of infinitude and finitude that relates itself to itself, whose task is to become itself, which can be done only through the relationship to God."[18]

The development of the self occurs through a kind of ongoing balancing act in which one attempts to not lose oneself in the abstract (infinitizing) or in the concrete (the mundane "material" of reality). To become a self is to achieve that happy balance of accepting the world (being content with finitude) but understanding that the ultimate criterion of one's life is eternity—defined by the God-relationship. When one relates to the eternal in this way, one has attained a "theological self," or a self whose "criterion is God."[19] As one writer puts it, "He becomes himself only by relating himself to God."[20] Selfhood, then, is both a responsibility and a process that culminates, for Kierkegaard, in an authentic embrace of Christianity, or what Kierkegaard also called "religiousness B."

The transition from religiousness A to religiousness B requires the interposition of divine revelation. Religiousness A is the sphere of immanent religiosity, or "pagan" religion, whereas religiousness B is the specifically Christian religion, defined by the particularity of the God-man.[21] God "deems it fit to become incarnate in time and history so as to effect an eternal happiness which even the most intensified inwardness could not achieve through its own efforts."[22] "Guilt-consciousness" (in religiousness A) is thereby disclosed as "sin-consciousness" (in religiousness B). The full theological truth of human selfhood and the human condition is existentially known and acknowledged, in the light of the revelation of Christ.

For Kierkegaard, human beings need divine revelation precisely—and simply—because they do not know what they need to know about themselves and their situation apart from it. Revelation is the suprarational disclosure or encounter of the divine with the human; revelation enters into the picture at the point where human rationality is lacking. This idea is the main theme of Kierkegaard's *Philosophical Fragments*, in which he

18. SUD, 30.

19 Kierkegaard explains, "This self is no longer the merely human self but is what I, hoping not to be misunderstood, would call the theological self, the self directly before God. And what infinite reality the self gains by being conscious of existing before God, by becoming a human self whose criterion is God" (ibid., 79).

20. Dupré, *Kierkegaard as Theologian*, 42.

21. Ibid., 561.

22. Schrag, "Kierkegaard-Effect," 10–11.

(through his pseudonym Johannes Climacus) articulates the difference between Jesus as revealer and Socrates as teacher. Because human beings are finite sinners, they need a teacher who imparts, through incarnation, the revelation of their sinfulness and their need for grace. Divine revelation is encapsulated in Jesus Christ; it is christocentric.

Which Is Better: Jesus Christ or Doctrines about Jesus Christ?

Kierkegaard affirmed the objectivity of Christian doctrine as well as the objectivity (in the sense of "facticity") to which doctrine points.[23] Nonetheless, the apex of revelation is *Christ*—the paradoxical God-man—who has acted in history and still meets us in the present; revelation is the disclosure in time and history of the person of Jesus Christ to individuals. This is Kierkegaard's notion of *contemporaneity*, which involves an understanding that while Christ's historical existence is crucial, what matters most (and what makes salvation possible) is a person's existential encounter with Christ. The title of the first chapter of Kierkegaard's lengthy discourse *For Self-Examination* is the question: "What Is Required in Order to Look at Oneself with True Blessing in the Mirror of the Word?" That question is answered in the title of the second chapter, "Christ Is the Way."[24] In order to have accessed divine revelation, one must relate contemporaneously to the God-man by faith and obedience. This begins, as Kierkegaard explains via Climacus in *Philosophical Fragments*, with the act of faith through which a single individual encounters God, as Christ, in a transformational experience he called the "moment."[25]

---

23. In a journal entry, Kierkegaard states, "The objective reality of Christ's atonement, independent of the subjectivity appropriating this to itself, is very clearly indicated in the story about the ten lepers. All of them were in fact healed, but 'Your faith has made you well' is said only of the tenth one, who gratefully turned back to offer God the glory" (*JP* 4, 4534).

24. *FSE*, 57.

25. Cf. Jan-Olav Henriksen's *The Reconstruction of Religion* for a helpful elucidation of the difference between Kierkegaard and Lessing (and most speculative philosophy) on the significance of the historical moment in time as a point of departure for religious belief and understanding. For Kierkegaard, Henriksen explains, the historical appearance of God to the individual in the gift of revelation through Christ is a contingent mediation, but one that is packed with existential relevance and salvific power (88–107).

For Kierkegaard, the contemporaneity of Christ is the reality of Christ in existential confrontation with a person. Revelation is not primarily the accessing and understanding of propositional or cognitive information; rather, it is a relational knowledge that effects a personal, spiritual transformation of the self. Divine revelation involves a personal, relational experience, an "encounter," rather than the acquisition of (merely) propositional, doctrinal knowledge or universal moral truths. To know Christ is to know the *person* of Christ rather than a doctrine *about* Christ, or even the teachings *of* Christ. As Kierkegaard's Anti-Climacus put it, "Christ is infinitely more important than his teaching."[26]

For Kierkegaard, the facticity (or historicity) of Christ's existence was crucial; this contrasted with much of the liberal theology that gained traction in the nineteenth century. In *Practice in Christianity*, Kierkegaard's Anti-Climacus asserted that the *fact* of Christ's existence is "the infinitely extraordinary, is the in-itself extraordinary."[27] However, the fact of Christ's existence cannot be proven by science or history (i.e., by objective methods). The claim of the facticity of Christ's existence (the eternal Son of God became, in real history, the God-man) causes the existential crisis of the question of faith: Do I believe or not believe? The *facticity* of the God-man's historical existence is the basis behind the existential (and salvific) significance that Christ's life provides the one who has faith. As one encounters Christ in the experience of subjectivity, one is presented with a choice: to have faith and believe (and accept the gift of forgiveness) or to "be offended."

The problem in Christendom was not that people did not believe in the objectivity reality, or facticity, toward which theological and biblical language pointed. Rather, the problem was that they did not interiorize, or appropriate, that language for themselves. In Christendom, Kierkegaard asserted, doctrine is "taken for granted." Christianity's concern should not be with arguments over doctrine, but with "giving the doctrine the ethical power over one's life which Christianity demands."[28] Instead, Kierkegaard averred, doctrine has become "a trivial matter to most people" and is "taken for granted." Kierkegaard wanted to see Christians subjectively interiorizing doctrine, or making the truth their own.[29]

---

26. *PC*, 124.
27. *PC*, 32. See also Walsh, *Living Christianly*, 68–69.
28. *JP* 4, 4544.
29. Ibid.

Knowledge of the person of Christ is too often equated, in conservative Christianity, with conceptual belief in doctrines (or a set of doctrines) about Christ or, in liberal Christianity, with knowledge about the historical (and moral) Jesus. Both can result in an intellectualizing and objectivizing of Christian faith. Certainly traditional evangelicals would be the first to proclaim that one's *relationship* with Christ is more important than cognitive, doctrinal knowledge. The primacy placed on cognitive assent to doctrinal formulations (i.e., confessions of faith), however brief they might be, raises the question of consistency between understanding and practice. Why is it, for example, that evangelical statements of faith emphasize doctrinal (cognitive) beliefs rather than the experience and practices of faith? Why do evangelical confessions of faith often lack attention to the ethical commands and discipleship orientation to which Christ invites us? Why are evangelism techniques so often focused on assent to doctrinal ideas *about* Christ?

In any case, Kierkegaard affirmed the significance of theology, but of a particular kind of theology—one that is subjectively oriented and that views the Bible as Scripture, a living book that communicates the living Christ. How could we know about this Christ apart from the Scriptures, which narrate his life? The Bible provides the initial information needed for the subsequent, *subjective* appropriation of essential truth; thus, for Kierkegaard, the Bible was clearly important.

EDIFYING WORDS: KIERKEGAARD'S VIEW OF SCRIPTURE

"The Bible lies on my table at all times and is the book which I read the most."[30]

On the whole, both Kierkegaard's statements about the Bible and his use of biblical texts reflect a high esteem for the Bible as the "word of God." Kierkegaard's regard for the Bible is especially pronounced in his signed religious discourses and in his journals, though even his pseudonymous writings give evidence of both a deep knowledge of Scripture and an appreciation for its transformative power. Kierkegaard often emphasized the New Testament's divine origin and its imperatival nature and was convinced

---

30. *SLW*, 230. Technically, these are the words of one of Kierkegaard's pseudonyms, but they reflect Kierkegaard's own appreciation for the Bible; he could easily have said this about himself.

that the Bible should function in an authoritative, normative way for Christians.[31] Kierkegaard viewed the Bible as divinely authoritative and as an edifying text, meant for the spiritual transformation and formation of its readers as they engage its central content, the God-man. The problem, in his view, was that the Bible's purpose had been forgotten.

In his later years, Kierkegaard's musings on the Bible were often connected to his perception that the Christianity of Denmark was far removed from the New Testament ideal. In Denmark, he charged, "We have a viewpoint flatly contrary to that of the New Testament, a completely different kind of eyes, so to speak." Christendom is so far from the Christianity of the New Testament that it is a "conspiracy" against it. "By nature man [sic] is against the Christianity of the New Testament." His final diagnosis, famously pronounced in his "attack upon Christendom" in his later years, was an unhappy one: in Denmark, "Christianity does not exist at all."[32]

The authority of the Bible derives from the authority of God. In submitting to the teachings of the Bible, the reader is submitting to God. Thus, even when its content might seem paradoxical, the required response is trust, obedience, and appropriation. Kierkegaard's incisive words rang out:

> [I]s it not a self-contradiction on your part that you accept Holy Scripture to be the word of God, accept Christianity as divine teaching—and then when you bump up against something which you cannot square with your ideas and feelings—then you say that it is a self-contradiction on the part of God, rather than that it is self-contradiction on your part, inasmuch as you must either dismiss entirely this divine doctrine or take it just as it is.[33]

Kierkegaard linked Christendom's lack of obedience to Scripture to the presumed hermeneutical sophistication of its leaders. In particular, he viewed the burgeoning field of higher criticism as emboldening the avoidance of the Bible's penetrating demands. As the practice of "higher" scholarship increased in prominence, a sense of God's active, providential involvement in history decreased, resulting in an increasing "spiritlessness" in the church. As he put it:

---

31. Timothy Polk notes, "In the vol. III entries [of *Kierkegaard's Journals*] it is primarily the satire on the way Christians seek to evade the claim of scripture upon them that attests Kierkegaard's high estimate of scripture's authority." *Biblical Kierkegaard*, 21.

32. *JP* 3, 2915.

33. *JP* 3, 2888.

> In our time scholarly doubt grows stronger and stronger and takes away one book after another. The orthodox give up hope. Remarkable! They assume that the New Testament is the word of God—but then they seem completely to forget that God still exists [er til].[34]

"Scientific scholarship" was, for Kierkegaard, mainly an excuse to avoid the strenuousness of the New Testament.[35] In a journal entry, Kierkegaard suggests that the New Testament should be read without a commentary. Using the analogy of a love letter, he wonders why anyone would read a love letter using a commentary.[36] The "love letter" metaphor sheds light on Kierkegaard's distaste for scholarly apparatus and third-party mediation. The Bible is written from God to the single individual and should be read with that in mind: "Every commentary detracts. He who can sit with ten open commentaries and read the Holy Scriptures—well, he probably is writing the eleventh, but he deals with the Scriptures *contra naturam*."[37]

It is important to note that Kierkegaard likely did not object to the use of critical interpretive methodologies as a basic hermeneutical tool, when used for the purpose of greater biblical understanding. But he objected to the elevation of human reason as the final arbiter of what the Bible means.[38] Most crucially, he objected to using higher criticism as an avoidance of or distraction from Scripture's ethical and religious function. The key, he insisted, was the disposition of the interpreter and the goal of interpretation.[39] Kierkegaard did not object to the application of reason (and imagination) in the interpretation of Scripture, nor did he object to people interpreting Scripture and doing theology; he was a Lutheran, after all.[40] His concern was to secure the priority of divine revela-

---

34. *JP* 1, 214.

35. On this point, see Rae, *Kierkegaard and Theology*, 45–46

36. *JP* 1, 210. He acknowledges that, were the letter written in a foreign language, one would learn the language in order to understand the letter, but otherwise use of a commentary should be out of the question.

37. Ibid.

38. Ibid.

39. One of the influences on Kierkegaard's theological education was the biblical scholar H. N. Clausen. Clausen was a student of Schleiermacher and a devotee of the "rational" and philological approach to synthesizing the Bible's meaning. See Elrod, *Kierkegaard and Christendom*, 31.

40. Kierkegaard's view of the Bible and of the freedom of individuals to interpret the Bible contrasted with N. F. S. Grundtvig, his contemporary, who argued that the best

tion *over* human rationality and to maintain a place for the Holy Spirit in guiding one's interpretation of Scripture.[41] Kierkegaard would rather see Denmark give all its Bibles back to God[42] than perpetuate a situation in which the Bible is approached as a historical curiosity, an aesthetic masterpiece, or even a doctrinal compendium, rather than for what it really is: the "highway signs" pointing to Christ, the way of truth and life.[43]

An important caveat is necessary to consider here. While the overall thrust of Kierkegaard's authorship and project reveals a trust in the Bible's authority, this trust is very different from *grounding* the Bible's authority, or even the epistemological truth of Christianity, in the Bible's historical veracity or textual perfection. Contrary to modernist orthodox understandings of the Bible, for Kierkegaard the Bible is not a secure epistemic foundation for Christian faith. The attempt to use it that way functionally eliminates the need for faith.

Kierkegaard noted the discrepancy between his view of the Bible and that of (modernist) orthodoxy: "They assume Scripture is inspired divine revelation," thus "there must be perfect harmony between all the reports down to the least detail; it must be the most perfect Greek, etc."[44] Kierkegaard suggested a different approach: "God surely knows what it means 'to believe,' what it means to require faith, that it means the rejection of direct communication, the positing of an ambiguity."[45] This led Kierkegaard to suggest that "because God wants Holy Scripture to be the object of faith and an offense to any other point of view, for this reason there are carefully contrived discrepancies (which, after all, in eternity will readily be dissolved into harmonies); therefore it is written in bad Greek, etc."[46] The Bible reflects the "ambiguity" of the real world and points away from itself

---

response to the rising critical, rationalist approach (and to the problem of interpretation) was to set the Bible aside in favor of the creeds and church practices. For a comparison of Grundtvig and Kierkegaard on the role of the Bible in the Christian life and church, see Roberts, "The Living Word or the Word of God?"

41. The role of the Spirit in biblical interpretation and theology will be unpacked in chapter 3.

42. *JP* 1, 216.

43. *JP* 1, 208.

44. *JP* 3, 2877.

45. Ibid.

46. Ibid. It seems odd to speak of God "intending" imperfections in Scripture; Kierkegaard's point is that God's provision of revelation did not necessitate the circumvention of the ambiguities of finitude.

to God. *Our faith is in God, not in the Bible.* The Bible's authority derives from its divine—not human—origin.[47] The mark of its authority is not its aesthetic beauty, poetic power, but in its religious and ethical force. It bears the marks of transcendence—to those who have ears to hear.

In a critical piece on the controversial Danish pastor Adolf Adler, who claimed to have been given a prophetic message from God, Kierkegaard distinguished between a "true apostle" and a "literary genius." The genius belongs to the category of immanence, while the apostle belongs to the category of transcendence; the two are "qualitatively different."[48] The simplicity of apostolic writing isolates and highlights the urgency of the message and the authenticity of its testimony as God's Word.[49] The writings of an apostle cannot be "proven." They can only be stated with conviction and a passionate appeal that the words truly come from God. Then it is up to the reader/hearer to decide what to do with it.[50]

C. Stephen Evans, noting a "link between subjectivity and authority," suggests that the authority of Scripture as the divine Word enhances rather than detracts from the principle of subjectivity in Kierkegaard's thought. Whereas many significant modern and postmodern figures tend to think of deference to authority as an unfortunate capitulation to externally imposed authority, Kierkegaard believed that the widespread failure to recognize the category of divine authority inhibited the development of genuine subjectivity and the development of the self. Evans states,

> Contrary to critics who see the two as opposed, the subjective individual is someone who has a foundation for the self that cannot be justified by appeal to the criteria embedded in the practices and discourse of the social establishment. Hence, the subjective individual is someone who is grounded in and at least implicitly appeals to a higher authority that provides that foundation.[51]

---

47. In another journal entry, Kierkegaard pointed out that the "bad Greek" of the New Testament corresponds to the social status of the apostles, "who were very simple men of the poorest class (for in this way their *authority* was all the more accentuated; they were nothing in themselves, not geniuses, not councilmen or state governors, but fishermen—therefore all of their *authority* was from God)" (JP 1, 182).

48. WA, 94.

49. WA, 96.

50. WA, 97.

51. Evans, "Kierkegaard on Religious Authority," 52.

Evans notes that for Kierkegaard, while it might be dangerous to be a subjective individual who relies on a religious authority such as a revelation, it is just as risky, if not more so, to be an objective individual who relies on a supposedly objective authority (such as human reason). The latter, in fact, is even more dangerous because it takes no account of the knowing individual's personality, reducing the knower to a "machine" for whom "inwardness is eliminated and genuine human life is simply abolished."[52]

This is perhaps the most challenging aspect of any claim to offer Kierkegaard as a "prophet" for postmodern Christianity. Kierkegaard's understanding of the importance of divine revelation and his attempt to recover the importance of its authority for the human life and experience cannot be molded to fit neatly the postmodernist ethos of the distrust of authority claims. Jean-François Lyotard famously described the postmodern condition as "incredulity toward metanarratives."[53] A metanarrative, or "grand narrative," is an explanatory narrative that presumably legitimates a particular discourse's (i.e., history, economics, science) interpretation of reality; this narrative is used to justify the often oppressive behavior of the community or group who owns the metanarrative. But is not the positing of divine revelation the ultimate claim to a metanarrative? Does not the claim of divine revelation lead to the suppression and oppression of the "other"? Perhaps Kierkegaard offers emergent Christianity some uncomfortable prophetic wisdom on this point. In their understandable reticence to assert ideological power over others, emergent Christians ought not to disregard the notion of divine revelation so central to Christianity. Doing so can lead to the flattening of faith, to a blurring of the uniqueness of the religions, and—more tragically—to a muting of God's voice in the world *and* in the church, culminating in yet another form of spiritlessness. Does emergent Christianity provide sufficient room for divine revelation to speak—even an uncomfortable word?

A doctrine of revelation is an unavoidably Christian notion. Furthermore, it is not necessarily contrary to the theologies of emergent Christianity. Kierkegaard's theology of revelation can cohere with the postmodern aversion to metanarratives, because it is deeply critical of modernist assumptions and is conjoined with a humble epistemology (more on that in chapter 2). Furthermore, revelation, for Kierkegaard, is centrally about a *subject to whom we are subjected*—the person Jesus Christ—rather

---

52. Ibid.
53. Lyotard, *Postmodern Condition*, xxiv.

than an ideology that can be mastered. Revelation eludes the grasp of the powerful, the wise, and the "winners" in history. It is for the weak, for the child. It is believable only through faith. Indeed, it *requires* faith to relate to it authentically. Those who wield divine revelation as a weapon never truly experienced it in the first place.

In a recovery of the essentially Christian, the doctrine of revelation ought not to be neglected. At the same time, however, Kierkegaard offers a way of understanding Scripture's authority that moves beyond the impasse of liberalism and conservative evangelicalism and that helps reorient an understanding of revelation in a way more conducive to the primacy of existential authenticity and to the intent of revelation to mediate salvation. Kierkegaard's prophetic word reminds us to get down to the business of obedience. Are we living in accordance with how God is speaking through the Scriptures? Are we hearing God *through* the Bible? Are we truly following Christ?

EDIFYING WORDS: FRAGMENTS OF AN EMERGENT THEOLOGY OF SCRIPTURE

It is high time to shift into a dialogue between Kierkegaard and emergent Christianity and the contemporary theologians who have influenced the movement. Like Kierkegaard, postmodern Christians understand divine revelation as deeply christocentric, thoroughly relational, and existentially transformational. Whereas liberal theologians often emphasize the human, historical side of revelation (Jesus as the true human being and the humanity—and thereby fallibility—of the Bible), conservative evangelicals emphasize the divine side of revelation (Jesus as *God* and Scripture as a *divine* book). Furthermore, conservatives tend to distinguish between the nature and purpose of the Bible: it *is* inspired, inerrant, infallible, *therefore* it functions to bring about transformation.

Emergent Christians strive to push beyond the dichotomies, viewing Christ's humanity and divinity (his human, historical life and his contemporary presence) as equally significant and the Bible as an intricate synthesis of divinity and humanity, the result of finite humans hearing and responding to the voice of an infinite God. Furthermore, for postmodern Christians, divine revelation is understood to be mysterious, deeply relational, and powerfully transformative. Contrary to the conservative evangelical distinction between nature and function (or purpose), Kierkegaard and emergent Christians realize that the Bible's nature is inextricably tied to its purpose: it is a divinely inspired book with sacramental, transformational power. But its transformational power does not hinge on any prior understanding of the Bible's nature (i.e., inerrant, infallible, etc.). The Bible *is* what it *does*. But what it *does* shapes our understanding of what it *is*.

The Bible, Epistemic Anxiety, and Emergent Theology

One immediate connection between Kierkegaard's view of revelation and emergent Christianity has to do with the modernist anxieties about epistemological certainty. Modernists aspired to know the *really real*, to have a firm grasp on "absolute truth." We will encounter the postmodern epistemological turn more fully in the following chapter, but for now it is worth noting that modernist anxieties about epistemic certainty impact our view of Scripture. As Kenton Sparks notes, modernists, in both liberal and fundamentalist streams, have an "inflated sense of epistemic certainty," whereby they assume that their (or their theological heroes') interpretations of the Bible represent the final position on the matter. For conservative evangelicals, this epistemic anxiety is seemingly repressed by an inordinate attention to the doctrine of inerrancy ("total truthfulness," or perfection in all that it communicates).[54] To assert "inerrancy" is to make a claim of epistemic supremacy for the Bible (though too often it means to make a claim for one's *interpretation* of the Bible). This leads some inerrantists to say things like, "when the Bible and science [or history, or sociology, etc.] conflict, I side with the Bible every time."[55] The foundational (epistemic) role for the doctrine of inerrancy, conceived in primarily propositional terms, reveals an unbalanced, disintegrated approach to revelation and a naïve epistemology.[56] Even evangelicals' own doctrines of Scripture necessitate some level of epistemic uncertainty. Take one prominent example: when fundamentalist evangelicals affirm the Bible's "complete inerrancy," they sometimes simultaneously acknowledge that the Bible is only actually (and completely) inerrant *in the original manuscripts*, which no

---

54. Sparks, *God's Word in Human Words*, 231.

55. I heard a prominent young-earth creationist assert this at a conference on "Origins." Of course, what is really going on is that when his *interpretations* of the Bible conflict with a scientific theory or scientific data, he goes with his *interpretations* every time.

56. See McGowan, *Divine Spiration*.

Reclaiming Revelation

longer exist. But, we may wonder, of what use is a doctrine of inerrancy for allaying epistemic anxiety when we do not have the inerrant texts?[57]

In Kierkegaard's view, God does not want us putting our faith in an "objective" document. God wants us to work hard at listening to him through Scripture and living our lives in faithful response to his paradoxical, indirectly communicated presence. God makes use of finite instruments (human authors, limited perspectives, fallible cosmologies, particular languages, etc.) to communicate his Word; this is a testimony to the goodness of the created order and to God's willingness to penetrate graciously—if not completely—through it.

In the Bible, we encounter the mystery of God. Through the "frailty" of human language, the divine secret is brought near. Peter Rollins, an important emergent thinker, notes that revelation is not primarily "that which makes manifest some otherwise hidden side of God"; rather, it "brings the hiddenness of God into close proximity with the individual."[58] God's mystery should not be minimized, undermined, or domesticated by engagement with Scripture. As Rollins suggests, the incarnation, which is at the heart of Christian faith and doctrine, affirms that God's mystery is intractable. For Rollins, the upshot is "that revelation is testified to in a radically subjective transformation. Not in the sense that it is somehow evoked by the subject, but in the Kierkegaardian sense of transforming the subjectivity of the individual."[59]

Many critics of emergent Christianity have worried about what they perceive as an explicit rejection of biblical authority, which they see stemming from the emerging church's "conversational" ethos.[60] Emphasis on

---

57. A more adequate (and more Kierkegaardian) understanding of inerrancy would frame inerrancy in terms of authorial intentionality, or the nature (genre) and intention of the communicative action implied through the text. A conception of "intentional inerrancy" seemingly lessens the epistemic anxiety brought about by the reader's observation of historical, scientific and other "imperfections" in the text, which are natural consequences of the text's original (ancient) context. Further, and more controversially, intentional inerrancy can also make room for a dyamic of divine, authorial intentionality as the reader engages Scripture in his or her contemporary situation. In an account of intentional inerrancy, emphasis lands on the adequate appropriation of the text's intended communicative action as well as the divine author's intentions regarding the transformation of the reader through the text.

58. Rollins, "Biting the Hand that Feeds," 82.

59. Ibid.

60. See, for example, Henard and Greenway, *Evangelicals Engaging Emergent*; DeYoung and Kluck, *Why We're Not Emergent*; and Carson, *Becoming Conversant*.

dialogue and insistence on validating multiple perspectives seem to preclude, to these critics, strong claims about truth and convictions about Scripture's authority. Furthermore, critics have worried about emergent leaders who depart from traditional or established interpretations of the Bible, deducing that, on the basis of theological creativity or diversion from inherited interpretations, emergent Christians have rejected the authority of divine revelation. Such worries, insofar as they manifest a genuine concern to maintain a doctrine of revelation and the authority of Scripture as an important component of that revelation, are worthy of consideration. It is feasible, however, that postmodern Christians do not reject either a role for revelation or a governing notion of the authority of Scripture; they may simply have a different conception regarding how biblical authority works—and differing interpretations of the meaning of biblical texts. Brian McLaren, a prominent representative of emergent Christianity, relates his own deep appreciation of the Bible and his respect for its authority:

> I have spent my entire life learning, understanding, reappraising, wrestling with, trusting, applying, and obeying the Bible, and trying to help others do the same. I believe it is a gift from God, inspired by God, to benefit us in the most important way possible: equipping us so that we can benefit others, so that we can play our part in the ongoing mission of God. *My regard for the Bible is higher than ever.*[61]

Such an emphatically stated claim for one's high regard for the Bible's authority ought to be taken very seriously—even at face value. The legitimate debate, of course, concerns how biblical authority plays out in theology and interpretation. Agreement *that* it is authoritative is quite different from agreement about *how* it is authoritative. For emergent Christians, it is conceivable that their view of authority stems from all or some combination of the following: (1) a recognition of the diversity of Scripture's forms (genres) and content, in particular the pervasive presence of poetic or highly image-based forms, such as narrative, poetry, and parable; (2) a view of Scripture as a *derivative* authority (God is the ultimate authority; the Bible is subservient to God and is instrumental, not an end in itself) that is subordinate to a christocentric view of revelation; (3) a *relational* view of Scripture's authority, in which the authority of the Bible is mediated through loving, gracious dialogue between text and reader (with the

---

61. McLaren, *Generous Orthodoxy*, 159. See Blount, "A New Kind of Interpretation," for his engagement with McLaren's hermeneutics.

purpose of building up rather than tearing down); and (4) a generous acceptance of the validity of multiple interpretations (even, perhaps, differing interpretations of the same biblical texts). It is important to suggest that emergent Christians do not reject the authority of divine revelation and of Scripture (as a component of that revelation). Emergent Christians are looking for a way to relate to this ancient text as authoritative, while living truthfully and authentically in the modern (or, rather, postmodern) world.

Biblical Authority beyond Literalism and Liberalism

Peter Rollins, in *The Fidelity of Betrayal*, reflects on the "fissures and conflicts" of the Bible, suggesting that they "are exactly what we expect to find from a purely human construction pieced together over such a wide expanse of time."[62] The Bible's "frailty," implied by the finite aspects of its composition, should quell our anxieties about applying the Bible literally. This does not imply, for Rollins, that "we can no longer testify to its divine status."[63] It does mean that recognition of the Bible's finitude, or "humanity," alleviates the pressures conservatives typically feel to harmonize, synthesize, and explain or cover over the "problems" in the Bible. Ironically, the marks of finitude in the Bible can become testimonies to its divine inspiration.[64] A similar slant on biblical authority is reflected in this statement by a recent emergent perspective on Scripture:

> The fact that the Bible must be read by finite and frail humans if it is going to be Scripture for anyone is one of the main reasons why we believe in its divine and authoritative nature. The inspiration and transformation of flawed communicators and the expression of transcendent truths despite the limits of human language are unmistakable markers of a divine presence.[65]

---

62. Rollins, *Fidelity of Betrayal*, 41.

63. Ibid., 41–42.

64. Rollins is not always consistent—or clear—in his writing on this issue. For example, he suggests (in the section quoted above) that the finitude of the Bible "counts against the idea that this work is anything other than human creation." And yet, he also affirms its "divine inspiration." Following Kierkegaard, I would press Rollins to speak more emphatically regarding the Bible's divine source and the imprint of divine authority, while also affirming Rollins' movement away from anxieties about epistemic certainty and biblical literalism.

65. Conder and Rhodes, *Free for All*, 71.

For emergent Christians, rather than undermining the divine authority of Scripture, the human or finite aspect (both of its authors and of its readers/interpreters) is a testimony to the remarkable "presence" of God in and through it—from its origin to the present day.

Walter Brueggemann, a major theological influence on emergent Christianity, puts quite succinctly, and in contemporary terms, a Kierkegaardian approach to the Bible. For Brueggemann, the literalism of fundamentalism and the (objective) historicism of liberalism trap the Bible in modernist categories; in consequence they mute its voice and squander its life-giving and prophetic power. In *The Book that Breathes New Life*, he suggests that the Bible is "fundamentally alien to modernity" and its "authority can never be articulated or summarized in dominant modes of rationality."[66] Literalism tries to "control" the Bible, while liberalism hopes "for a kind of benign distancing that this restless book will never tolerate." When the Bible is rightly approached in communities of faith, both the Bible's "terror" and "healing power" are preserved.[67] Both are essential.

Scot McKnight, another influential voice in the emergent/emerging dialogue, suggests that rather than focus on terms of attribution (inerrancy, inspiration, etc.), which he calls an "authority approach," we should follow a "relational approach" to the Bible.[68] Words like *authority* and *submission* do not aptly describe, he says, his own experience of reading the Bible. The relational view includes those elements but goes well beyond them, into the experience of delight and love. McKnight notes that "the relational approach *distinguishes God from the Bible*. God existed before the Bible existed; God exists independently of the Bible now. God is a person; the Bible is paper. God gave us this papered Bible to lead us to love his person. But the person and the paper are not the same."[69] McKnight concludes his reflections on Scripture thus: "Let me put this now one final way: God gave the Bible not so we can know it but so we can know and love God through *it*."[70]

In a similar vein, Debbie Blue, a co-pastor of House of Mercy, an emergent community in St. Paul, Minnesota, notes that the God of the Bible is not controllable and predicable (like an idol) but dynamic, challenging,

---

66. Brueggemann, *Book that Breathes New Life*, 18.

67. Ibid., 19.

68. McKnight, *Blue Parakeet*, 87. McKnight was at one point in time an important ally for the emerging church; he remains an influential figure in the progressive wings of evangelicalism.

69. Ibid.

70. Ibid., 91.

and perplexing. The Bible, she says, calls us into relationship with God, leading us into a "tangle." Too often, we readers work hard to get ourselves out of the tangle, when in fact the tangle is precisely the point.[71] Echoing a common theme, she notes, "We're dying for certainty and stability and a firm place to stand. But believing that's what we have in the Bible, the Word of God, we mistake the summons of the living God for a rock, and our relationship to scripture looks more like idolatry than a living response to a living being."[72] For Blue (and reminiscent of Karl Barth), God is not confined to a book. The Bible, as a witness to the reality of God, does not so much "contain truth" as function as "a vehicle for experiencing the Word of God." But the Word of God, she says, is "what happens in the struggle" between the reader/hearer and the living God. The Scriptures witness to the living God, such that these words on the page of Scripture "somehow, oddly, live."[73] Rather than look to the Bible to "fix things for us" or make our difficult decisions for us, we must live in a relationship with a God we cannot control. The Bible is a "witness" to that God.[74]

A critic responding to this view of Scripture might wonder why the Bible cannot both "contain truth" (even *propositional* truth) and facilitate an encounter with the living God. After all, we would surely allow that all sorts of books contain truth; why not the Bible too? If the Bible is not just any other book but is uniquely given to us by God, why should we not expect truth—even the propositional kind—from the Bible? Nonetheless, one should consistently ask *what kind of truth one is encountering* when reading or preaching a particular text, so as to not expect something of the Bible that it is not designed or intended to give. The issue that Blue, McKnight, McLaren, and others are rightly pressing is that one should not replace the truth of the living God ("visibly" centered in the person of Christ) with the written words, the locutions, of the Bible. We have to get the order right: God, *then* Bible. The purpose of the Bible is to lead us toward authentic, relational, existential knowledge of God. Yet Kierkegaard's emphasis on the distinctive nature of the Bible's origin, a "love letter" from God, reminds us that the Bible deserves reverence and attention for its transformational content and its divine origin—as well as for what often happens when readers "subjectively" engage it for appropriation.

71. Blue, *From Stone to Living Word*, 32.
72. Ibid.
73. Ibid., 42.
74. Ibid., 35–36.

Community of Interpretation and Action

Walter Brueggemann has rightly noted that in our context, "the question of authority must be posed anew, because the categories of the conversation have shifted." The authority of revelation can no longer be thought of in terms of either logical ("scholastic") proof or a purely romantic approach to experience, "or as a probe into scientific categories." Instead, we have to consider "what it means to be a community of interpretation and action called into existence by a text that remains distant and of less utility in the pursuit of certitude."[75] The Enlightenment quest for certainty cannot be carried over in a post-Christian, postmodern, postcolonial world.

The way in which Scripture will speak to us as communities and as individuals will depend upon our situation, our context. Subjectivity determines the existential and shapes the theological import of Scripture's claims upon the reader. The Spirit takes up the Scriptures to help us understand its significance and its imperatival force in our lives. Christians cannot (indeed, dare not!) rely on academic theories of inspiration or inerrancy to determine whether or not the Bible is authoritative before they act on its authority. Rather, the "authorizing power" of the Bible is "of another order."[76] What are we to do with it? How are we to respond to it? These questions will be pursued more fully in the following chapter as we engage the question of the intersection of interpretation (hermeneutics), theology, and the imagination.

Conclusion

Kierkegaard's understanding of divine revelation and his approach to Scripture challenges the ways in which evangelical and liberal theology often highlights (though in differing ways) rationality, certainty, universality, and objectivity with respect to God's revelation in Scripture. In dialogue with emergent theology, it opens us up to a more dynamic and a more "living and active" relationship to the Word of God. It encourages us, in our work of interpreting, reading, translating, and theologizing, to listen for the voice of God. What is the Spirit saying to the churches? It just might liberate us to live more in the freedom of the gospel.

---

75. Brueggemann, *Book that Breathes New Life*, 5. Brueggemann writes, "The authority of scripture can be understood only in relation to and in terms of the communities it authorizes. The authorizing power of the text is evident through both its demand for obedience and its grant of permission to act in new ways against both accommodation and oppression" (16).

76. Ibid.

Chapter Two

AGAINST CERTAINTY

"[F]rom the demonstration nothing follows for me; from faith everything follows for me."[1]

KIERKEGAARD'S INFAMOUS PHRASE, "TRUTH *is subjectivity*," suggests that the essentially Christian is oriented by personal concern for truth and passionate engagement in the process of knowing.[2] Christian truth cannot be appropriated via objectivity; objective approaches betray an overreliance on finite, cognitive knowledge and suggest that contextual subjects can grasp the world and know truth purely and in totality. The appropriation, or authentic assimilation, of religious and existential knowledge demands a subjective stance toward it: a *shift* to the subjective mode. The knower must be concerned about the relevance and impact of it on one's life. Kierkegaard emphasizes the *How*-nature of subjectivity over the *What*-nature of objectivity. This involves a transformation in understanding what it means to be a human being. Kierkegaard took to task—to the woodshed, even—the modernist emphasis on self-sufficiency, universal reason, disinterested reflection, and logical certainty.

---

1. *CD*, 191.
2. "Subjectivity is truth" and "truth is subjectivity" are key phrases occurring throughout *Concluding Unscientific Postscript*.

Kierkegaard's epistemological turn to subjectivity involves a shift from a preoccupation with objective certainty to existential passion for and personal involvement with truth. Consequently, he was against the classical apologetic approach: using "objective reason" to attempt to rationally prove the validity of Christianity or the existence of God: "[F]rom the demonstration nothing follows for me . . ."[3] For Kierkegaard, an approach to truth based on disinterested "observation" or even logical argumentation that relies on rationality as the criterion for the legitimacy of Christian faith leads to an idolatrous reduction of the essentially Christian to the categories of human rationality. Human reason becomes the arbiter of the truth of divine revelation and the determiner of the validity of religious experience. In effect, the mind becomes the *master* rather than the servant. For Kierkegaard, the validity of religious experience hinges on the existential struggle that accompanies subjective appropriation—and that gives rise to a deeper longing for God. In Kierkegaard's Christian theology, he means a particular kind of appropriation, which results from a personal encounter with God in Jesus Christ. The subordination of human rationality in the appropriation of Christian truth is fitting, if only because the incarnation is beyond the reach of human reason (for Kierkegaard, it is the thought that "thought itself cannot think.")[4] That paradox of the God-man elicits the passion of faith, because it lies outside the boundaries of mere human reason. An implication of Kierkegaard's turn to subjectivity is that objective certainty of religious knowledge is not only unattainable, it is undesirable. Objective certainty of the deepest matters (the religious, the existential) would diminish the vibrancy of religious commitment and would undermine the need for faith. This implication of Kierkegaard's epistemology might be difficult to swallow, both for many evangelical conservatives and for skeptical rationalists alike, but it seems to resonate with emergent Christianity.

THE SHIFT TO SUBJECTIVITY: PASSIONATE, PERSONAL INTEREST IN THE TRUTH

> To exist subjectively with passion (and it is possible to exist objectively only in absentmindedness) is on the whole an absolute condition for being able to have any opinion about Christianity.

3. *CD*, 191.
4. *PF*, 37.

Anyone who is unwilling to do that and yet wants to have anything to do with Christianity, whoever he may be and however great he may be, is in this matter essentially a fool.[5]

Kierkegaard's notion of subjectivity (the notion that *truth is subjectivity* and *subjectivity is truth*) is the idea that every person's highest task is to develop as a self; that is, a person who inwardly appropriates truth and, in so doing, rightly relates to God, to others, and to oneself (and is thus a theological self).[6] By making the truth his or her own, one lives in accordance with what one believes to be true. The significance of the development of selfhood means that the truth appropriated is not merely true; it is the highest, or deepest, truth accessible to human beings. In other words, it requires the appropriation of Christian truth—centered in the absolute paradox that the Son of God became the God-man, the eternal God incarnate in historical time. The appropriation of the truth of Christianity precludes objectivity because God cannot be made into an "object." God is *subject* who confronts us in time and history.

Kierkegaard's *Philosophical Fragments* and *Concluding Unscientific Postscript to Philosophical Fragments* lay the foundation for and provide an explanation for his thesis that "truth is subjectivity." In these works, Kierkegaard's pseudonym, Johannes Climacus, aims to discover an answer to the question, "Can an eternal happiness be built on historical knowledge," and if so, how?[7] Christianity, Climacus says, "wants to make the single individual eternally happy"; but the question remains as to how this might actually happen—and whether this might actually occur in his own life. Climacus concludes that the question of one's eternal happiness relates to the subjective issue of Christianity, that is, "the individual's relation to Christianity."[8] The issue, considered objectively, is the question of the "truth of Christianity"; but its truth, objectively speaking, has no impact on a person's salvation—nor does it evoke the subjective passion necessary for appropriation. Eternal salvation comes through subjectivity, which, as we have seen, is the possibility of the appropriation of Christian truth, and thus

---

5. *CUP*, 280.

6. Kierkegaard writes, "to become subjective should be the highest task assigned to every human being, just as the highest reward, an eternal happiness, exists only for the subjective person or, more correctly, comes into existence for the one who becomes subjective." *CUP*, 163.

7. *CUP*, 15.

8. Ibid.

of acquiring eternal happiness. "Truth is subjectivity" means that a person must inwardly appropriate Christianity for it to be *truth-ful*. Subjectivity is both a way of knowing and a way of being—and the being and the knowing are interconnected as a task that one undertakes.[9]

For Kierkegaard, the truth of Christianity cannot be abstracted from existence—and therefore from people who appropriate and embody it (followers of Christ). Therefore, the main question is not about the doctrine or the truth of the doctrine as such, but rather about the way in which one relates personally to the doctrine: whether in belief, trust, and obedience, or skepticism, doubt, mere intellectual curiosity. As he states, "truth has always had many loud proclaimers, but the question is whether a person will in the deepest sense acknowledge the truth, will allow it to permeate his whole being . . ."[10]

Like Augustine, for whom *faith seeks understanding*, Kierkegaard believed that true religious knowledge of Christianity required a passionate orientation toward it. Understanding, knowledge, and the passion of existence go together. Thought cannot be divorced from practice. Kierkegaard intriguingly suggested that if Pilate had been passionately oriented, "he would never have let Christ be crucified."[11] That is, had he been subjectively related to truth, he would have recognized that Jesus *is* the truth. He would have responded personally and existentially to the personal encounter with the God-man. Instead, Pilate represented the objectivity of the age, whereas Jesus reflected subjectivity to the highest degree. In other words, Pilate represented the religiously apathetic state of the situation of Christendom.

As we have seen, Kierkegaard increasingly attempted to expose the religious apathy and hypocrisy in Danish Christianity. In one of his discourses Kierkegaard described the crucial difference between possessing knowledge *about* Christianity and inwardly appropriating that knowledge:

---

9. David R. Law, in his "Kierkegaard on Truth," points out two ways Kierkegaard uses "subjectivity is truth" in *Concluding Unscientific Postscript*. He suggests the first meaning of the phrase is the individual's *relationship* to the truth, and the second meaning is the individual's *being* in the truth (subjectivity is a *way of being*). The difference has to do with how one is related to something *outside* oneself and with how one does (or does not) reflect truth inwardly, in one's own life. Law states, "If the individual relates him- or herself correctly—i.e., with passionate commitment to the truth—then that individual is in the truth, even if the object to which the individual relates him- or herself is not the truth" (104).

10. *CA*, 138.

11. *CUP*, 229.

> Everyone who lives in Christendom ordinarily has received more than enough information about Christianity (even the government sees to that); many perhaps have received all too much. What is lacking is certainly something entirely different, is the inner transformation of the whole mind, by which a person in life-peril of the spirit comes in earnest, in true inwardness, to believe at least something—of the considerable Christianity that he knows.[12]

The key, for Kierkegaard, is not how much theological knowledge one has, but whether or not one appropriates and "reduplicates" that knowledge (transitioning knowledge from merely conceptual understanding into ethical-religious action). When it comes to objective knowledge about Christianity, sometimes less is more.

This leads us to an important caveat. Kierkegaard, via Climacus, recognized that objective approaches to knowledge in various academic discourses (e.g., history, philosophy) are valid, so long as objectivity was kept in its proper place and only when the "object" of knowledge could be adequately known through objective approaches.[13] Even Christianity, Climacus noted, can be considered from an objective point of view. But this is conceptual knowledge, not the personal and existential knowledge of subjective appropriation. Christianity is subjectively oriented; it is related "essentially to existence," which means that it has immediate, direct bearing on how one understands oneself and the meaning of one's life.[14] Existence is a constantly flowing stream that the thinker cannot step out of in order to "see the whole" from an objective, or eternal, standpoint.[15] Thus the one who subjectively appropriates Christianity approaches life (and the pursuit of truth) as a quest—not for objective knowledge, but for authenticity, passion, and obedience to God. To restrict oneself to asking about the objective truth is to remain in the mode of speculation, where (objective) knowledge does not affect one's life.[16]

---

12. *CD*, 245–46.
13. *CUP,* 21.
14. *CUP,* 199.
15. "But the subjective thinker is an existing person, and yet he is a thinking person. He does not abstract from existence and from the contradiction, but he is in them, and yet he is supposed to think. In all his thinking, then, he has to include the thought that he himself is an existing person" (*CUP,* 351).
16. Climacus notes, "The inquiring, speculating, knowing subject accordingly asks about the truth but not about the subjective truth, the truth of appropriation. Accordingly, the inquiring subject is indeed interested but is not infinitely, personally, impassionedly

None of this means that knowledge about faith is impossible or that we never come to know anything related to religious faith with personal conviction. Rather, it means—for one thing—that knowledge is never complete because existence is never complete. It also means that objectively speaking, despite the passion of one's religious convictions, one could always be "mistaken." Christ was a historical being. But history lies outside of the realm of the provable. The Bible mediates, in part, our objective (and narrative) knowledge of God and Christ. But the Bible cannot be proven to be absolutely historically factual, objectively speaking. There can be no objective "proof" for the viability of Christianity; objective certainty about the religious is elusive. Human beings cannot step outside of their limits (geography, history, language, etc.) and attain a universal perspective on reality. When *God* is the issue of knowledge, one's relation to the subject matter is best (and religiously speaking, *only*) approached through the passionate subjectivity of faith—not through objective reflection. As we have seen, Christianity is an "existence-communication"; it cannot be truly understood apart from existing in it and without being deeply, personally transformed by it.[17]

FAITH, KNOWLEDGE, AND A DIFFERENT KIND OF CERTAINTY

Faith, for Kierkegaard, is made possible by the contradiction between the infinite passion of inwardness and the confrontation with objective uncertainty. If we were able to apprehend God objectively (as we might apprehend the intricacies of electrical engineering), we would not have faith. But since we cannot, faith is requisite to knowledge of God. In order to continue to have faith, we must hold on to the objective uncertainty, even in the presence of its apparent absurdity. We find ourselves "out on 70,000 fathoms of water," floating on a sea of objective uncertainty; therefore faith is required.[18] Authentic religious existence is characterized by a continual *striving* that recognizes that its task can never be finished in this life. Having understood this reality, however, faith presses on and gains a kind of

---

interested in his relation to this truth concerning his own eternal happiness" (*CUP,* 21). Kierkegaard elsewhere states, "A mature person learns only by appropriation, and he appropriates essentially only that which is essential to living" (*CD,* xv).

17. *JP* 1, 517.
18. *CUP,* 204.

convictional assurance through praxis and the experience of relatedness to God.

John Heywood Thomas, in *The Legacy of Kierkegaard*, points out that Kierkegaard critiqued modernist rationalism from a deeply theological standpoint. Kierkegaard was adamantly against modernist (specifically Hegelian) interpretations of Christianity, which purported to provide an "interpretive key" to the Christian religion through philosophical categories or—even further—attempted to supplant the particularities (and offenses) of Christianity altogether with rational philosophy. As Heywood Thomas notes, "Rationalism, [Kierkegaard] came to believe, was confusion. It represented the union of Christianity and philosophy, the result of which was the confusion of language."[19] For Kierkegaard, issues of faith "have to be dealt with on their own terms," and faith itself offers a critical resource for philosophical reflection—not as something philosophy can explain, but as a distinct, if complementary, discourse. Rationalism, as an "objective" enterprise, is of minimal use in this quest; it can stunt or even nullify the development of faith when it becomes an idol. An essential element of Kierkegaard's epistemology is that faith is not simply another kind of rationality, or a variation of rationality; rather, faith has its own kind of logic—its own mode.[20]

Kierkegaard sought to disabuse modernists of the notion that rationality has a supreme place in human "knowing" and can therefore usurp the role of faith, even in religious knowledge. Kierkegaard was very much against what we today call "classical apologetics," or the attempt to prove the existence of God by recourse to human (neutral or objective) rationality. Contra the impulse of natural theology and "proofs" for God's existence, Kierkegaard's Climacus noted that the "works from which I want to demonstrate his existence do not immediately and directly exist, not at all."[21] Even when it seems that the "wisdom in nature and the goodness or wisdom in Governance of the world [is] right in front of our noses," we are confronted with the "most terrible spiritual trials here." In other words, the temptation to doubt is still present because the existence of God does not follow "from the demonstration." Consequently, Climacus (and Kierkegaard) rejects natural theology as a rational proof for God's existence.[22]

19. Heywood Thomas, *Legacy of Kierkegaard*, 57–58.
20. Ibid., 68.
21. *PF*, 42.
22. *PF*, 42.

For Kierkegaard, apologetics, in this sense, simply borrows from the methods, presuppositions, and values of Enlightenment rationalism. Classical apologetics operates under the assumption that human rationality is universal and that objectivity is possible, even in matters of deeply paradoxical realities (e.g., the incarnation; the Trinity; the nature of God and the "infinite qualitative distinction between time and eternity"; the elusiveness of religious language, etc.). Furthermore, Kierkegaard suggests, every attempt to rationally prove God's existence is in effect a backhanded insult to God, "an attempt to make him ludicrous."[23] If God really exists, he does not need our arguments on his behalf. So to argue *for* God's existence is counterproductive; it is, in a sense, a sign of the weakness of belief. Furthermore, it suggests that God is an objective *thing* rather than a divine Subject who is subjectively encountered and cloaked in mystery.

On matters that should concern human beings the most (religious ones), epistemological certainty—in the objective sense—eludes us. Nonetheless, a kind of certainty is possible: a certainty available to human subjectivity. We might call this a *psychological* or *psycho-religious* certainty. One can have a kind of personal conviction that accompanies a serious commitment to religious belief. People often deeply commit themselves to religious beliefs. These religious commitments are accompanied by a profound *confidence* driven by one's subjective passion; this epistemological confidence often issues forth as emotional or psychological certainty, which differs from the lazy, unflinching objectivity of epistemological certainty. Indeed, passion is the mark of subjective involvement. Objective knowledge does not inspire such passion; more often than not, it precludes it. The deeply paradoxical realities (i.e., the God-man) that lie at the center of Christianity inspire the passion of subjectivity rather than the measured coolness of objective rationality and certainty. The key is to distinguish epistemological confidence from epistemological certainty; the former allows for a parenthesis (i.e., "But I could be wrong"), which is a more optimal stance than epistemological certainty, given both the faith-nature of Christianity and our current context of postmodernity.

Stephen Emmanuel helpfully situates Kierkegaard's epistemology in the *pragmatist* tradition associated with William James.[24] For James and the pragmatists, the situations in which persons seek after truth (and the kind of truth they are seeking after) should be accounted for in the

---

23. *CUP*, 545.
24. Emmanuel, *Kierkegaard and the Concept of Revelation*, 52–55.

methods and manner in which that truth is sought. History and science might require objective methods, but religious knowledge requires the passion of faith. Doubt (skepticism) and trust (faith) are differing postures with respect to the mysterious realities of religion—either way, the position one takes is "an expression of will."[25] So, consistent with the pragmatist tradition, Kierkegaard "questions whether objectivity provides an appropriate model for thinking about important issues of ethics and religion."[26] Belief, desire (and human need), and commitment are interconnected. As we have observed, Kierkegaard believed that Christianity is deeply connected to human desire: primarily, the desire for *eternal happiness* (salvation). Furthermore, it is centered in the paradox of the God-man, which requires passion (personal, emotional, volitional involvement) in order to believe it—or to believe it *subjectively*. The paradox elicits further passion, desire, and commitment in the person who chooses to follow Christ. We do not approach truth objectively and dispassionately, but subjectively and from positions of existential concern. We desire truth. We desire to know. Contrary to the assumptions of modernism, the connection of truth and knowledge with personal involvement is not a hindrance to progress, but an essential precondition for it.

This personal, pragmatist notion of truth is not a capitulation to relativism or hermeneutical nihilism (truth is not, contrary to how it might sound, "whatever we want it to be"). Rather, from the perspective of Christianity, the criterion of our theological beliefs and religious convictions are the fruits they bear. Further, truth and knowledge are the results of a pursuit of individual and communal longing *to know and to understand.* Faith seeks understanding, but faith is not grounded on neutral, "rational" knowledge, historical proof, or logical or scientific verification: "From the demonstration nothing follows for me; from faith everything follows for me."[27] Faith is its own ground. Our beliefs are driven and shaped by God-given desire. This means that, in the realm of faith, truth is subjectivity. Objective proof will get you nowhere. It will certainly not get you to God. Perhaps (objective) doubt is not faith's enemy, but its friend; perhaps it is simply the other side of faith.

Postmodernity invites an injection of humility into epistemology. This carries over into all arenas of knowledge and every discourse. In our day

25. Ibid., 55.
26. Ibid.
27. *CD*, 191

it is generally acknowledged that subjectivity runs all the way down, from the religious to the scientific. Philosophers of science such as Thomas Kuhn and Michael Polanyi have alerted us to the personal element and subjective dimensions involved in the sciences.[28] Kierkegaard was not attuned to this full reach of subjectivity, because in modernity the sciences operated under a presupposition that complete objectivity and universality were possible: the "pure" scientific method. Were Kierkegaard alive today, I doubt he would be surprised by the pervasive acknowledgment of the reach of subjectivity, even in the hard sciences.

Critics of emergent Christianity should take this growing acceptance of the depth and reach of human subjectivity in the acquisition of knowledge and the character of truth to heart. Emergent thinkers are not so much driven by relativism or by relativist impulses; rather, they have recognized and assented to the deep reality of subjectivity as an inherent component of the human condition, as a natural characteristic of the knowing process, and as a recognition of the personal (and existential) nature of Christian truth. We simply do not have access to a "God's-eye view," an objective view from eternity.[29] However, in Jesus Christ, we can have personal "contact" with ultimate truth. The human shape of epistemology is perhaps the most significant lesson postmodernity has taught us, but it is one we could have learned from St. Paul: "We see through a glass, darkly" (1 Cor 13:12).

THE PLACE OF DOUBT IN FAITH: KIERKEGAARDIAN EPISTEMOLOGY FOR EMERGENT CHRISTIANITY

It is probably no exaggeration to say that the central issues dividing proponents of emergent Christianity from its critics are epistemological ones. That is, critics seem to be primarily concerned not so much with the material content of what emergent Christians believe (though some have concerns there, too); rather, they seem most concerned with the underlying structure and presuppositions about what it means to have knowledge

---

28. As philosopher of science, Michael Polanyi has argued that passionate concern and subjective involvement with a matter is not a detriment to the acquisition of knowledge, even in the hard sciences. Rather, it is a crucial motivator for scientific discovery. See his highly influential *Personal Knowledge*. My first introduction to Michael Polanyi's work came through Esther Meek's *Longing to Know*. See also her lengthier and more recent book, *Loving to Know*.

29. What Kierkegaard called a view of reality "*sub specie aeterni*"—"from the perspective of eternity" (*CUP*, 308–9).

and, in consequence, what it means to do theology. Postmodern Christians have been generally comfortable with epistemic uncertainty, ambiguity, and indeterminacy. They have tended to see knowledge and theology as an important part of the journey, but as bearing the marks of the process nature of the existential quest. The questing ("striving") approach to the Christian faith causes theological heartburn to many critics of emergent Christianity. If we cannot know theological realities with epistemic certainty, then this means that we cannot be certain that we know God, we cannot trust the Scriptures to be true (inspiration, inerrancy, etc.) or uniquely authoritative, and we cannot honestly claim that Christianity is more true than any other religion or that Christ is the only savior. So what are we to make of these questions?

We cannot address each of these questions here. But it is clear that Kierkegaard accepts the ambiguity and the anxieties that such questions raise. They cannot be answered—in a "case closed" sort of way—because to answer them with objective certainty would be to undercut the primacy of faith and of subjective appropriation for the essentially Christian. A Kierkegaardian perspective on epistemology lends empathetic support to the postmodern sensitivity to the inevitability of ambiguity, epistemic uncertainty, hermeneutical plurality, and—ultimately—to the process (or quest) orientation of theological knowledge.[30] Kierkegaard, as we have seen, warns people against trying to buttress their faith by appeal to some external, objective knowledge. Confrontations with the paradox of the God-man forces either an embrace of the paradox, in which one appropriates the revelation and submits to the living Christ, or a rejection of it. Any other approach minimizes the paradox and suppresses or minimizes the passion of faith. To minimize the paradox is to needlessly buy into the assumptions of modernism, or to place logic and rationality over the raw facticity of the God-man. This does not mean, however, that there is no role to play for rationality. Kierkegaard's view of faith is not irrational; rather, it is *suprarational*.[31] The difference is that at some point human rationality, logical discourse, and intellectual explanation must make room for the transcendent, existential, subjective experience of faith.

---

30. This is not meant to imply *process theology*, which would invite a different conversation.
31. See Emmanuel, *Kierkegaard and the Concept of Revelation*, 39–46.

The Postfoundational Orientation of Emergent Christianity

The story of the modernist quest for certainty begins with the pervasive influence of what is now often called *classical foundationalism*. Enlightenment modernists were impelled—some might say impaled—by an anxious desire to establish the rationality of, or justification for, their beliefs. Belief had to be *justified*, or sufficiently warranted, to count as true belief—and therefore as *knowledge*. To be considered knowledge, a belief had to be based on impeccable evidence and shown to be self-evident, infallible (unquestionable or indubitable), and indefeasible (impervious to critique). These epistemic foundations were required to be "non-inferential" or *basic*; that is, they did not derive their justification from other beliefs. They were the bedrock upon which other derived beliefs rested and from which they drew their epistemic support. The candidates for foundational beliefs could range from empirical observation, to experiential perception, to rational deduction. The appeal of classical foundationalism to the modernist project is clear: it matched the tenor of the Enlightenment mood of optimism in knowledge and seemed to hold at bay an undercurrent of epistemic anxiety. Do I *really* know? How can I know *that* I know? The classical foundationalist project involved the attempt to gain epistemic certainty and to shed the baggage of beliefs that contained the seeds of doubt.

The heyday of classical foundationalism is long past; the collapse of modernist optimism corresponds to its demise, such that one can hardly find any classical foundationalists today. As Merold Westphal states, "That it [classical foundationalism] is philosophically indefensible is so widely agreed that its demise is the closest thing to a philosophical consensus in decades."[32] In its strongest, classical form, foundationalism is now widely considered to be an impossible ideal. Most philosophers and theologians recognize that not all of our beliefs can be justified infallibly or indubitably; further, most acknowledge that our beliefs (and the "knowledge" we claim to have) are situated within deeply historical, inescapably human (and therefore fallible), constantly changing contexts. We must adjust to the reality that our beliefs and our knowledge are context-dependent. To rationally justify all our beliefs, from the mundane to the sublime, is both impractical and impossible.

Imagine justifying, to the degree of rationality required within classical foundationalism, that driving your car on a busy freeway in Chicago is

---

32. Westphal, "Reader's Guide to 'Reformed Epistemology,'" 11.

a safe enough prospect. Now, imagine you had to go through that epistemic process every day before you began your commute.[33] That seems easier, however, than rationally justifying—with the epistemic certainty required by classical foundationalism—that Jesus Christ is God. Some beliefs, whether mundane or existentially profound, require basic acceptance and trust—and that should be enough. As finite beings, we cannot overcome the "infinite regress" of justification by chasing down rational support for all our beliefs. Sometimes "just knowing" and *experiencing* that the sandwich is sitting there in front of me, that the car will not fall apart on the highway, and that Jesus Christ is Lord, is all the justification one needs—unless confronted by resounding evidence to the contrary. This kind of justification does not come with epistemic certainty, however, and is contingent upon the truth of the matter. A tire just might burst on the highway, and the atheists *could* be right: God might be a fiction of our collective imaginations. Ultimately, we have to admit that absolute certainty about the truth of even our most cherished beliefs requires eschatological verification; in other words, only time will tell.

For many conservative evangelicals, retaining some version of foundationalism is important because the idea of "absolute truth" is important. Conservative evangelicals often fear the specter of epistemic relativism, employing ominous phrases like "truth decay" to refer to the cultural shift into postmodernism.[34] Foundationalism offers a standard of rationality (even if the relation between that standard and the power and privilege of those policing it is too often overlooked) that purports to transcend "mere" experience or personal perception. Truth is absolute, knowledge is not a matter of human construction, and belief is either rational or irrational. The affirmation of an infallible foundation seems, at first glance, to fend off relativism. In the words of Francis Schaeffer, one has access to *true truth*.[35] This impulse is understandable, given the history of neo-evangelicalism

---

33. Classical foundationalism fell out of favor in part because of impracticality (we simply do not and cannot live in accordance with the ideal of infallible, rational justification for all knowledge), but also because its own basic tenets could not be rationally justified to the degree of certainty required. The very possibility of infallible beliefs and "self-evidence" of truth came under deep suspicion.

34. See Groothuis, *Truth Decay*. Note also the title of David Wells' influential book, *No Place for Truth: Or, Whatever Happened to Evangelical Theology?*

35. Schaeffer, *He Is There and He Is Not Silent*, 42. For a discussion of Schaeffer's religious epistemology in comparison to Kierkegaard's, see my essay, "Francis Schaeffer: How Not to Read Kierkegaard."

as an alternative to modernist liberalism and as a more culturally and theologically sophisticated version of modernist fundamentalism. For foundationalist-minded evangelicals, the Bible is often considered to be the infallible foundation of our theological knowledge. Foundationalism and a particular view of biblical authority, in which the Bible's authority equals their interpretation of it, often fit hand in glove.[36] In other words, "the Bible 'says' it and I believe it." What the Bible "says," is objectively determinable through the application of adequate interpretive methods.

A growing population of *modest* foundationalists within evangelical (and other) ranks spurns the quest for unflappable, apodictic certainty that so consumed their classical forebears. They affirm the reality of foundations (some beliefs are more *basic* or more foundational than others), but insist these beliefs need not bear the marks of self-evidence, infallibility, or indefeasibility to be considered rational (and justifiable) beliefs. A modest foundationalist, for example, may admit that while the Bible is—for the Christian—a foundational source of belief and knowledge, one's *interpretation* of the Bible is not infallible. Thus, even if the Bible is considered to be inerrant and infallible, our epistemic access to it is not.

In his defense of modest foundationalism, Michael Rea argues that postmodernists too often conflate the various forms of foundationalism by ignoring the difference between "doxastic" and "source" foundationalism.[37] Source foundationalism (which is basically classical foundationalism) is "the view that some of our sources of evidence are privileged in the sense that (a) they can rationally be trusted in the absence of evidence of their reliability, and (b) it is irrational to rely on other sources of evidence unless they are somehow 'certified' by the privileged sources."[38] In other words, source foundationalists isolate and then privilege one or several sources of knowledge (e.g., empirical observation or rational deduction), which are then considered to be self-evident, indefeasible, and infallible.[39] A foundational source is thought to be a fail-safe justifier of belief; other, derived beliefs are justified as being true knowledge insofar as they adhere to—or follow from—the source. Doxastic foundationalists, on the other

---

36. This view of biblical authority is also typically grounded in a heavily propositional approach to theology and a disproportionate reliance upon historical-grammatical hermeneutics.

37. Rea and Crisp, *Analytic Theology*, 12–17.

38. Ibid., 13

39. Rea names empiricism and rationalism as two primary examples of source foundationalism.

hand, simply recognize that some of our beliefs are more foundational than others.[40] These beliefs can be considered properly basic without *also* being self-evident, infallible, or indefeasible. They exert influence on our actions, behaviors, choices, and other beliefs; we come to expect that influence, so long as those beliefs continue to function for us as basic. The key difference between doxastic foundationalism and its classical counterpart is that the former is a *humbler* version (*doxastic* means "opinion"). It seems safe to say, though, that many conservative evangelicals at least *function* as "source foundationalists"; the shadow of classical foundationalism still hovers. Infallibility (and inerrancy) is presumably channeled from the source (the Bible, or experience, or reason) to one's belief. The problem with source, or classical, foundationalism is that it excludes—either naively or brazenly—the limitations and contextuality of the human experience from the equation.

Alvin Plantinga's "Reformed epistemology" is an influential example of modest foundationalism in Christian theology.[41] For Plantinga, belief in God constitutes a "properly basic" belief; it requires no further elaboration or justification for the person holding that belief to be adequately *warranted* in believing it. Just as I believe that this coffee cup is sitting there in front of me, or that I love my wife and children, I believe in the existence of God. To be warranted in believing something like the existence of God does not mean one has access to a *positive,* apologetic argument through which others will be convinced of theism. It simply means that at some point in the line of questioning, deduction, or argumentation, the infinite regress must stop; it does so at the point of these properly basic beliefs, and as long as one follows adequate protocol for virtuous thinking, one is reasonably justified in *trusting* the basic belief. A theist who has experienced God's reality (via, say, the *sensus divinitatus*) should be under no particular burden to justify her belief by recourse to additional evidence—no more burden, in any case, than an atheist should feel in justifying his conviction that there is no God.

---

40. Jim Beilby ("Contemporary Religious Epistemology") notes that doxastic foundationalism is simply the recognition that some of our beliefs *anchor* our other beliefs.

41. Interestingly, Rae suggests that Reformed epistemology, which "admits religious experience, or something like a special faculty for producing religious beliefs . . . as an additional basic source of evidence," might be characterized as "a move in the direction of a brand new source foundationalism" (*Analytic Theology*, 16). This seems right: Reformed epistemology could count as either doxastic or source foundationalism, contingent on whether one's religious experience (the *sensus divinitatus*) is perceived to be an indefeasible, epistemic source for belief in God.

Reformed epistemology can result in epistemic humility: I believe in God, and I believe I am justified in believing in God, but that is as far as I will go. I will not presume that *you* or anyone else *should* or *must* believe in God on the basis of evidential reasons outside of your experience. On the other hand, it can also result in epistemic certainty and unflinching dogmatism. The crucial factor is whether one views one's religious experience as self-evident, infallible, and indefeasible—or not.

C. Stephen Evans has suggested that Reformed epistemology has some striking parallels with Kierkegaard's religious epistemology.[42] For Kierkegaard, the way of classical foundationalism is a dead end. The Enlightenment attempt to establish, with epistemic certainty, the foundations of all belief and knowledge by isolating thought, or rationality, is wrongheaded.[43] Furthermore, the classical apologetic approach to proving the existence of God is fundamentally misguided.[44] Evans suggests that faith, for both Plantinga and Kierkegaard, is "epistemologically basic." For Kierkegaard, there is no rational or evidential *ground*, or justification, for faith. As human beings, we do not occupy the perspective of eternity; we cannot escape our subjectivity in order to construct an objective, "view from nowhere," eviden-

---

42. See his essays "Kierkegaard and Plantinga on Belief in God" and "Externalist Epistemology, Subjectivity, and Christian Knowledge."

43. While Kierkegaard disagreed with Descartes' approach (and even more emphatically with those who followed in his wake), he had some appreciative things to say about him. For Kierkegaard, Descartes' flaw was to privilege thought over being and to assume that thought comes before being, existence, or *act*, and that it is possible to abstract oneself from existence by thinking. For Kierkegaard, it is impossible to abstract oneself from existence; thus, a person's *will* is a more fundamental reality than reflection. To doubt is an act of the free will, which means that the process of thinking is an ethical activity of real persons within actuality. The only end to the infinite regress of reflection (doubting) lies in the act of the *will*—thought bends to action, not the other way around. For Kierkegaard, it is "not *cogito ergo sum* but I act *ergo sum,* for this *cogito* is something derived or it is identical with 'I act' . . ." (JP 3, 2338). In another journal entry, he says, "Doubt is certainly not halted by the necessity of knowledge (that there is something one must acknowledge) but by the categorical imperative of the will, that there is something one cannot will. This is the will's concretion in itself, by which it shows itself to be something other than an ethereal phantom" (JP 2, 1244).

44. Kierkegaard suggests that "God can no more prove his existence by way of something else than he can swear; he has nothing higher than himself to swear by" (JP 2, 1314). And again, "The idea of proving the existence of God is of all things the most ridiculous. Either he exists, and then one cannot prove it (no more than I can prove that a certain human being exists; the most I can do is to let something testify to it, but then I presuppose existence)—or he does not exist, and then it cannot be proved at all" (JP 2, 1334).

tial argument for a mysterious, divine reality. After all the arguments and counterarguments have been given, the only justification for faith in God is *faith itself*. Faith is experiential, not theoretical; it pertains to the sphere of subjectivity rather than speculation and rationality.

Evans makes a convincing case for the commonalities between Plantinga and Kierkegaard on the knowledge of God. Plantinga, however, is primarily interested in articulating the notion of *warrant* for our beliefs. Given Plantinga's concern with warrant, it seems that his epistemology can go either in the direction of epistemic humility or epistemological arrogance. Not so with Kierkegaard. As such, a better comparison can be made between Kierkegaard and *postfoundationalism*, which attempts to move beyond the either/or dilemma of nonfoundationalism and foundationalism; it avoids the former's relativism and latter's obsession with grounding and warranting belief. Postfoundationalism acknowledges the contextuality of our beliefs (for Kierekgaard, belief and knowledge come out of *subjectivity* and *actuality*, not the other way around) and of our knowledge (including what have been presumed to be "objective" fields, like scientific knowledge), but it does not collapse into mere contextualism, subjectivism, or relativism, as one might find in nonfoundationalism.

The influential postfoundationalist J. Wentzel van Huysteen commends an interdisciplinary, or transdisciplinary, understanding of rationality that embraces our embeddedness in social, cultural, biological, and all other contexts.[45] He suggests that postfoundationalism allows us to "move beyond the epistemological dichotomy of foundationalist objectivism and nonfoundationalism."[46] Thus, rather than reject the possibility of truth and rationality (as nonfoundationalism does), postfoundationalism pursues an interdisciplinary and "cross-contextual" dialogue (i.e., theology and science) in pursuit of truth. The cross-disciplinary quest for truth involves dialectic between, and even "fusion" of, epistemology and hermeneutics.[47] The turn to hermeneutics underscores the contextuality of knowledge and truth; *we must interpret reality*. But to interpret well, we need to utilize shared sources of rationality and interdisciplinary conversations. While Kierkegaard did not explicitly acknowledge subjectivity in the scientific disciplines (as he did with religious belief), his perspective resonates with

---

45. Van Huyssteen, *The Shaping of Rationality*. See also his *Essays in Postfoundationalist Theology*.

46. Van Huysteen, *Shaping of Rationality*, 8.

47. Ibid., 13.

van Huyssteen's recognition that epistemology itself is a deeply subjective and hermeneutical discourse (since subjectivity implies interpretation). Belief and knowledge are necessarily situated within the context of passionate, human and creational life. Like Kierkegaard, postfoundationalism underscores the *process* whereby we seek after truth and the lived, ethical aspect of the rationality of belief.

At this point, I should acknowledge that the line between *doxastic* or modest foundationalism and postfoundationalism seems, at the surface level, very thin. Both modest (doxastic) foundationalists and postfoundationalists acknowledge that some beliefs, experiences, etc., function as more foundational than others. In practice, doxastic foundationalism could seem very similar to postfoundationalism. It is difficult to see why modest foundationalists of the doxastic sort need to retain the descriptor "foundationalism" at all. Granted, modest foundationalists could argue the converse—if some beliefs function more foundationally than others in our belief structures, why not retain the term? From the perspective of the (responsibly) postmodern critique, however, modest foundationalism still invites the epistemological equivalent of a "final answer," thereby perpetuating the anxious quest to justify belief. How do I know—I mean *really* know—what should legitimately count as a *properly basic belief*? Do not some properly basic beliefs seem remarkably nonbasic—and even disturbingly wrong—in hindsight? When it comes to belief in the existence of God, do not Darwin, Freud, and Marx each have sophisticated explanations for why belief in God seems so natural and so prevalent and so, well, *basic*? And do not neuroscience and neuropsychology offer us some very detailed, physical insight into the nature of "basic" religious belief? This is not to say that theism is untenable or unjustifiable (I am a convictional, committed Christian). But the characterization of "properly basic" as a strategy for epistemic justification does not get us very far. For Kierkegaard, not "getting very far" in epistemologically supporting, or warranting, religious faith is not necessarily a problem. In fact, faith is better off when it is not reliant upon rationality.[48] I agree with Evans when he suggests that, if Kierkegaard is a fideist, he is a "responsible" one; subjectivity does not license irrationality. Nonetheless, it is difficult to imagine Kierkegaard being ter-

---

48. Kierkegaard, reflecting on the work of one of his theological heroes (the German Lutheran Pietist J. G. Hamann), says that he has an idea in common with Hamann that he (Kierkegaard) has developed "out of a whole given philosophy and culture and into the thesis: to comprehend that faith cannot be comprehended or (the more ethical and God-fearing side) to comprehend that faith must not be comprehended" (*JP* 2, 1599).

ribly impressed by an extensive, intellectual attempt to rationally articulate *warrant* for religious faith.[49]

Postfoundationalism accepts the epistemic limitations and the inextricable interconnections of *all of* our beliefs, without giving up on the search for knowledge and truth and without denying the meaningfulness of "rationality." But in the human experience, belief, conviction, knowledge, and truth are deeply intertwined within the subjectivity of experience and context. *What a tangled web we weave.* Furthermore, epistemic justification is ultimately an eschatological reality—our beliefs will be proven or disproven *after* our temporal, finite situation reaches its end.

Many emergent Christians would likely reject foundationalism (perhaps even in its chastened or modest forms) because of their postmodern recognition that knowledge is contextually shaped and beliefs are interconnected within a larger system of beliefs, experiences, and *practices,* none of which can be cleanly isolated from the others. But they would also likely reject nonfoundationalism, because of its association with a totalizing relativism (or, if they do not reject it, perhaps they should consider doing so). On what basis would one continue to believe in the divinity of Christ or the authority of the Bible, for example, if all religious perspectives were thought to be merely internal worlds of (irrational) thought and experience, with no invitations for external critique and with no aim toward universality and trans-rationality?

When the theological leaders of the emergent movement imagine how beliefs are formed and either sustained, strengthened, or rejected, they likely think more in terms of a "web of belief," with interlocking and perhaps even seemingly random threads, rather than an upright (and uptight) structure housed on a single, solid, unassailable foundation.[50] This seems consistent with how emergent Christians approach questions of truth and theological knowledge generally. Their view of knowledge justification is probably more consistent with "coherentism," a philosophical position that asserts that the strength of the entire "web of belief," composed of related but distinct interlocking strands, comes from the aggregate coherence of

---

49. Evans, "Externalist Epistemology," 204.

50. Stanley Grenz, a formative influence on the early emergent movement (or at least postmodern expressions of Christianity), famously employed the metaphor of the web—or in his case, the "mosaic"—in his theology. See "Articulating the Christian Belief-Mosaic," 108. See also Grenz and Franke, *Beyond Foundationalism.* Moreover, Brian McLaren's notable emergent text, *Generous Orthodoxy,* is highly suggestive of a postfoundationalist epistemology underpinning his theological and ecclesial identity.

the web rather than from any of the individual threads.[51] Why do you believe Jesus is God? Because you trust the Bible. Why do you believe the Bible? Because you believe in Jesus (and because you have had profound spiritual experiences as a result of encountering the Gospels) and because the faith tradition through which you "learned Jesus" is itself deeply formed by Scripture. Our beliefs, interpretations, and theological convictions are inextricably interrelated in such complex ways that dissecting, analyzing, deconstructing, and reconstructing them takes serious work; it is a never-ending process—a quest, even. And sometimes the best thing we can do is to stop the endless rationalizing, let faith be faith, and let our living guide our thinking.

From Naïve Realism to "Creative Anti-Realism"

We have been discussing the question of the *justification* of knowledge (foundationalism, modest foundationalism, and postfoundationalism). But this is not yet to encounter the question of the *nature of truth*—the larger issue of whether "truth" is something human beings can actually access or legitimately claim to have attained. Naïve realists say that the very nature of the concept of "truth" suggests an optimistic outlook: human beings can have direct access to that which is true. Naïve realism holds that the world "out there" is accessible to our minds and can adequately be described through human language (and concepts). In short, the naïve realist suggests that what we observe, when our senses are properly functioning and when we are employing the right methods, is in fact truth (the *really* true). Many modernists are realists in this sense, because they believe that reality can be ascertained either through the exercise of deductive reason (rationalists) or through empirical observation and scientific induction (empiricists). Christian modernists often believe that we can ascertain the absolute truth of God by the objective, inductive observation of the "facts" of the Bible (induction is equated with interpretation—though occasionally deduction may also be necessary). Merold Westphal describes the modernist impulse or realism this way:

> with the help of biblical revelation we can achieve a knowledge of God wholly on a par with God's own self-knowledge. Our knowledge does not extend as far as God's, of course, but what we know

---

51. The epistemologist will note that the "coherence" view, based on the metaphor of the web, can also be utilized within a foundationalist perspective.

is not in any way inferior to God's knowledge of the same truths. This means that theological knowledge, with the help of revelation, achieves the ideal of objectivity and perfect correspondence that science was thought to achieve in relation to nature. This knowledge is entirely free from prejudice or perspective, is wholly unconditioned by interests and desires, and is relative to human culture.[52]

Westphal acknowledges that modernists are "fallibilists"; they understand that they do not have a God's-eye view on every matter, nor are they themselves inerrant in their interpretations of Scripture and in their understanding of reality. However, they believe that when they grasp truth (to whatever extent they have it), they grasp it *absolutely*. And their understanding of reality and their handle on that truth is essentially the same as God's.[53] For evangelical modernists, this conviction preserves the significance of divine revelation, the primacy of theology (we are *actually, adequately describing God when we talk about "him"*). In the modernist outlook, not only is there such a thing as "absolute truth," but we can have it *absolutely*.

But this modernist epistemology is, from the perspective of postmodern theology, deeply problematic and—in terms of preserving the notion of divine revelation and the active, motivated pursuit of truth (even truth about divine realities, including God)—unnecessary. The source of this problem is that modernist epistemology does not recognize the import of *subjectivity* with respect to our knowledge of God. For Kierkegaard, passionate, personal subjectivity is the only way to authentic knowledge of God.

In contrast to naïve realists, antirealists assert that while there is surely a reality "out there" apart from human minds, no human being will ever have any sort of actual contact with that reality such that they can claim possession of absolute truth. So for antirealists, there may well be a "God's-eye view," but human beings—as finite—do not have access to it. Divine revelation can cut through the fog (somewhat) and provide some insight that opens one up to experiencing, perceiving, and "knowing" something

---

52. Westphal, *Overcoming Onto-theology*, 78.

53. Westphal puts the matter thus: "What is known in this way is perfectly known. Not even God could know it any better. There is thus good reason for Kierkegaard's religious postmodernism and Nietzsche's atheistic postmodernism to agree in identifying their target as the claim to know *sub specie aeterni*." Ibid., 82.

truly, but antirealists insist that while we might (conceivably) know some things *that* God knows, we can never know anything *as* God knows it.

Postmodernists are deeply skeptical that reality can be simply "read off," or observed and restated by the human mind in this seemingly untainted way. Rather, reality is at least to a very large degree "constructed." People, both individually and collectively, participate in this construction of reality through an intricate and delicate combination of experience, observation, interpretation, synthesis, and conversation (dialogue). "Reality" (and therefore "truth") is constructed as much as it is discovered. How can we *really* know which is which?

In this antirealist perspective, human beings do not have objective, untarnished access to what is "real." If this is so with respect to the physical, natural world, how much more so with respect to the "unseen" divine realities that metaphysics and theology purport to describe? Westphal's "creative antirealism" proposes a "hermeneutics of finitude." Borrowing from Kierkegaard, he suggests that human beings cannot know the Truth about reality (employing the capital *T* to designate "absolute truth," or the "God's-eye view"), but they can know truth (small *t*). That is, their grasp of Truth (capital *T*) is emphatically and consistently constrained by finitude. He states, "the truth is that there is Truth, but not for us, only for God."[54] Westphal warns against the conservative Christian (modernist) impulse to "make their systems the repository of absolute truth" by which they "claim divine sanction for institutions that are human, all too human." When they do this, "They become more modern than biblical."[55] I would add here that the danger is equally possible for modernist liberals, for whom skepticism reigns supreme and knowledge is often determined by human reason. Creative antirealism opens up a more biblical relation to the idea of truth, allowing for the humility and openness implied by a biblical view of humanity and of God.

Westphal's "theologically motivated appropriation of postmodernism" suggests that when we speak about God, we should keep in mind that "the divine character of revelation does not cancel out the human character

---

54. Ibid., xvii. He clarifies further: "The truth is that there is Truth, but in our finitude and fallenness we do not have access to it. We'll have to make do with the truths available to us; but that does not mean either that we should deny the reality of Truth or that we should abandon the distinction between truth and falsity. Moreover, the most we should claim for this claim itself is that it is true, that it is the best way for us humans to think about the matter." Ibid., 87.

55. Ibid., xvi.

of my attempt to say what it means."[56] Thus, antirealism signals the "end of metaphysics" (insofar as metaphysics purports to give us a pure, objective understanding of God) and invites the project of "overcoming ontotheology"—the modernist attempt to objectively describe the being of God. In Westphal's words: "For just as I do not become purple by speaking about violets, so I do not become absolute by speaking about God."[57]

For Westphal, as for Kierkegaard, reality (and truth) is linguistically mediated. This means that, in terms of understanding how we access and describe reality, epistemology gives way to hermeneutics. We are always already caught up in language; reality is linguistically mediated. There is no pure, universal, objective language. All we have are finite, situated, "contextual" perspectives, shaped by necessity through the finitude of speech and limited by the ambiguities of translation.[58] Divine revelation is mediated through language; therefore, even revelation is filtered through the ambiguities of finitude. God has Truth, but he gives us truth. But truth is enough to know God—experientially, relationally, and redemptively.[59]

Is Critical Realism a Better Option?

Critics of emergent Christianity have homed in on their insistence upon epistemological humility. They argue that while humility is obviously a Christian virtue, one dare not be too humble about one's theological convictions; this would be suggestive of kinks in the armor of the Bible or Christianity and could ultimately lead to the denial of the faith altogether. Furthermore, perhaps one can be personally humble *and* epistemologically certain.[60] Detractors are concerned that the priority of the "journey" motif

56. Ibid., 79.

57. Ibid.

58. Westphal: "every language is . . . a particular conceptual scheme or vocabulary and lacks the universality that Truth requires." And again: "Every language is contingent in the sense that it contributes to our interpretation of the world elements which derive from historical accident rather than from super-historical, direct encounter with the real." Ibid., 83.

59. *CUP*, 118.

60. DeYoung and Kluck chide emergent Christians for emphasizing authenticity and *questing*: "I'm not advocating stuffing all our feelings, but we must learn that self-expression and being true to ourselves are not the surest guides to Christlikeness. Sincerity is a Christian virtue, as is honesty about our struggles. But my generation needs to realize that Christianity is more than chic fragility, endless self-revelation, and the coolness that

and the highlighting of epistemic humility will undermine the "knowability of God."[61] Particularly for the Reformed evangelical strain of critics of emergent Christianity, God's sovereignty can be seen in God's ability to make known truth about himself to humanity. That sovereignty is diminished if doubts are raised as to whether what has been revealed can be known truthfully (or rather, Truthfully). Some would urge that, in light of these criticisms, perhaps there is a "middle ground" that allows for greater epistemological certainty than the postfoundationalist, antirealist perspective.

Critical realism lies between naïve realism and antirealism. Critical realists assert that human beings can have partial, mediated access to reality and can have some confidence that their articulations of reality are truthful (though not complete, or perfect). On the critical realist account, knowledge claims fall between objective ("absolute") certainty and postmodern humility. The location on the spectrum depends on whether one puts the emphasis on *critical* or *realist*. In a book that gives a "lay of the land" of the future of the emergent church from various perspectives, Kevin Corcoran argues that emergent Christians need not, and in fact should not, embrace epistemic "creative antirealism" (i.e., Westphal's postmodern Christianity). Instead, he says, a robust critical realism will do the trick just fine.[62] While "Christian rationalism" is a failed project, epistemic humility simply requires the assertion of genuine "creatureliness," which is already deeply embedded in the Christian tradition.[63]

Corcoran is worried that antirealism is an extreme (and unnecessary) capitulation to postmodern relativism. I wonder, though, if Westphal's version of creative antirealism does not alleviate the worries that critical realists have regarding Christian appropriations of antirealism. As another scholar notes, Westphal simply highlights the crucial distinction between the (knowing)

---

comes with authenticity" (*Why We're Not Emergent*, 33).

61. Ibid., 35.

62. Corcoran, "Who's Afraid of Philosophical Realism?," 4.

63. "The claim that our grasp of reality is always partial, incomplete, and fragmentary, and the humility, tolerance, and dialogue that flow from such a realization do not require a corresponding commitment to creative antirealism. A firm grasp of our *creatureliness*—from which follows the fact that we humans are finite, frail, and fallible—I contend is sufficient in itself to engender a robust sort of epistemic humility. . . . [T]here is therefore no need to embrace the creative antirealism so often associated with postmodernism when the resources for epistemic humility are present in the Christian tradition itself." Ibid., 12.

subject and the perceived (known) object.[64] There is a "reality," but that reality is colored, filtered, and inescapably influenced by the context of the knowing subject. The doctrine of sin has long shaped the way Christians have thought about our perceptions of reality—but too often we forget that sin (and simply finitude) affects our noetic capacities, as well. Regardless of whether one is a critical realist or an antirealist, it seems to me crucial to make the move into a postfoundationalist account on the justification of our beliefs as "knowledge." Making this move, from epistemological certainty to confidence, secures the sort of epistemic humility that seems best suited for authentic witness in a postmodern and pluralist world.

Doubt as a Friend of Faith—and of the Church

The creative antirealist and postfoundationalist perspectives allow for a constructive role for doubt in Christian faith and theology. Doubt is the other side of faith: it is a friend, not an enemy of faith. The presence of and acknowledgment of doubt allows for the maturation of individual development. It facilitates the kind of existentially authentic faith I am advocating in this book. Furthermore, it allows—at the communal level—for the intellectual maturation of a church. A church that honestly, openly, and seriously engages the reality of doubt as a part of faith could be fertile soil for existential authenticity and spiritual growth. This ethos may be one of the defining features of emergent Christianity—the willingness to countenance doubt. These doubts can arise from questioning the sincerity of religious faith (e.g., Freud's "great apologetic challenge" to Christianity), the truthfulness of the Bible, the exclusivity of Christianity, or engaging in philosophical challenges to core Christian doctrines (such as those posed by the "problem of evil and suffering").[65] The acceptance of a positive role for doubt in the Christian life is consistent with the emergent ethos. Because emergent Christianity is not terribly anxious about epistemological certainty, such questions are encouraged—or at the very least accepted and engaged. Furthermore, there is no rush to answer the questions in a final, authoritarian way. This openness to the reality of doubt in the Christian journey need not imply a glorification of doubt nor a complete disregard for objectivity (properly placed) in Christian theology.

64. Laughery, "Evangelicalism and Philosophy," 259–60.
65. On Freud and the "great apologetic challenge" to the church today, see Beck, *Authenticity of Faith*, 15–24.

Emerging Prophet

A good case study here is found in the work of emergent theologian Peter Rollins. Rollins, who is quickly becoming one of the seminal thinkers of emergent Christianity, highlights an important function for doubt. If any emergent thinker might be guilty of glorifying doubt and disparaging confidence in belief, it is Rollins. However, he nuances quite delicately the relationship between doubt and belief in his book *Fidelity of Betrayal*. There he says that

> the truth spoken of within the Judeo-Christian tradition transcends the mundane level of debates concerning the accuracy of certain historical claims. . . . [T]his does not in any way mean that parts of the Bible do not make historical, geographical, and archaeological assertions, but rather that the real kernel of Christianity is referring to something infinitely deeper, richer, and more esoteric than some factual claim that can be accepted or rejected without any significant change in the individual.[66]

Rollins here references Kierkegaard's notion of subjectivity, noting that truth is transformative, not an "object of [objective] contemplation."[67] He insists this is not an "affirmation of doubt above all." Rather, the experience of doubt is an inevitable consequence of engaging reality. Acknowledging doubt prevents the *repression* of the existential angst that so often accompanies religious convictions. In this sense, doubt is not a sign of inauthentic (or weak) faith so much as a sign of authentic faith—or at least a sign of a desire for authenticity. Rollins suggests that doubt is "intimately tied up with faith, because the deep truth of faith gives birth to doubt."[68] Nonetheless, there is, for Rollins, an element of certainty available to the believer who embraces a postmodern form of Christianity; this is not the modernist, epistemological certainty of Enlightenment philosophy (rationalism or empiricism), but the certainty that something (the Word) has broken through our reality. As he concludes,

> Christian faith teaches us, if we are sensitive and able to be taught, that seemingly opposite and opposed realms of doubt and absolute certainty are reconciled in a knowing beyond knowledge. There is no doubt for the believer that God dwells with us (as an event), yet

---

66. Rollins, *Fidelity of Betrayal*, 117–18.
67. Ibid., 117.
68. Ibid., 142.

there is a deep uncertainty about who, what, or even if God is (as a being).[69]

Doubt must be seen as simply the other side of faith, as natural to the experience of knowing and experiencing God. Our theologies ought to reflect the finitude of humanity in light of God's infinitude and mystery. In another work, Rollins states, "in contrast to the modern view that religious doubt is something to reject, fear, or merely tolerate, doubt not only can be seen as an inevitable aspect of our humanity, but also can be celebrated as a vital part of faith."[70] For Rollins, the certainty that accompanies the subjectivity of faith also recognizes that we must progress beyond "onto-theology" into an existentially oriented faith that responds to the experience of God in the event of believing—the event of encountering God (divine revelation) in the context of our finite historical lives. In a similar way, Brian McLaren has consistently urged Christians to reject "absolute and arrogant certainty about our theologies" so as to retain a "proper and humble confidence in God."[71]

An epistemologically humble approach to theology and faith allows for deeper authenticity and for the deconstruction of the idols of certainty, dogmatism, and closure. Experimental psychologist Richard Beck asks, "What would religious faith look like, experientially and theologically, if it were not engaged in existential repression or consolation?"[72] Presumably, that kind of faith might be open about the reality of doubt and would courageously struggle with existential questions regarding the attainment of "truth." That kind of faith would not try to rely on or use religion instrumentally to assuage existential anxiety, but would attempt to be existentially authentic in the face of the lack of epistemological "objective" certainty; it would be open and honest about the pain and distress involved in the human experience and would not try to suppress the anxieties that arise from the fragmentation, brokenness, and brevity of human life. Collectively, in terms of the experience of Christian community, it might have the character and courage to deal head-on with pain, sorrow, and longing, even in (or especially in) the context of church liturgy. It would engage the Bible with seriousness and honesty, neither avoiding its prophetic strangeness nor minimizing its hermeneutical ambiguities, from the perspective

---

69. Ibid., 144.
70. Rollins, *How (Not) to Speak of God*, 34–35.
71. McLaren, *Adventures in Missing the Point*, 43.
72. Beck, *Authenticity of Faith*, 125

of the modern world. It would utilize both celebration and lament as representations of the full nature of the human experience. Ultimately, it would find both discomfort and solace in the central figure of Christian faith: the paradoxical God-man, who makes comfortable faith impossible but who alone can make authentic faith possible.

It means then that faith—and the theological knowledge that accompanies it—is more fragmentary, in reality, than systematic. It is more contextual than universal. It is more contingent than necessary. It is more mysterious, experiential, and subjective (in the Kierkegaardian sense) than logically precise and cognitively "manageable." When it comes to the doctrine of God, emergent Christians are more prone to emphasize the cognitive elusiveness and mysterious immensity of God than to assume they have direct, propositional access to the nature and mind of the divine. Emergent Christianity, by and large, is empathetic to the mystical and apophatic traditions of theology, those that emphasize the cognitive elusiveness of God; they are drawn toward the experiential and relational knowledge of the divine.

Conclusion

Kierkegaard provides postmodern theology and the emergent church a deeply Christ-centered perspective on truth, knowledge, and faith that does not capitulate to the errors of modernism. It encourages a humble epistemology, facilitating relationships of openness toward "the other"—a crucial move for the effectiveness of witness in our increasingly pluralist world. The emergent church can apply Kierkegaard's pragmatism in epistemology to free us from the "constraints" of modernist criteria (objective, dispassionate, rationalistic, etc.) and to unleash subjective passion for the discovery of truth and the creative engagement of the imagination with divine revelation. Kierkegaard's prophetic voice on the nature of truth and religious knowledge, with his turn "against certainty," resonates with the sensibilities of postmodern, emergent Christianity. He rightly advocates a turn toward the confidence and conviction inspired by the christological paradox that God has become a single individual in time. This approach to Christian life and faith invites a quest toward authenticity of self, genuine religious passion, a constructive exercise of imagination, and the unconditional love of neighbor. It is a quest that is not driven by the need to be right, the desire to win arguments, or by an exclusive or superior attitude. Rather, it is driven by a sense of gratitude for God's pervasive grace and the priority of divine forgiveness—themes we explore in subsequent chapters.

Chapter Three

RECLAIMING IMAGINATION

"When all is said and done, whatever of feeling, knowing, and willing a person has depends upon what imagination he has."[1]

KIERKEGAARD, AN EMERGING PROPHET, can help us reclaim a vital place for the imagination in the Christian life, especially with regard to how we read and interpret the Bible. This emphasis contrasts with the two forms of modernism we have been navigating: conservative evangelicalism and liberalism. Both approaches, from their differing theological presuppositions, stake too much on objectivity, either the "objective meaning" of the Bible (conservative evangelicals) or the "objectivity" of science, reason, and moralism (liberals).

Conservatives are overly optimistic regarding the use of theological and interpretive methodologies (such as "grammatical-historical exegesis") to arrive at "absolute truth." They operate on assumptions about the capacity of human language to accurately (though, to be fair, not *exhaustively*) mirror divine reality. Liberals have the reputation of historicizing and *demythologizing* the Bible in order to extract its "real message," or its moral/ethical teachings, bypassing the often perplexing nature of biblical texts and the challenging particularity (and offense) of the gospel message.[2] Like

---

1. *SUD*, 31.

2. On the strange bedfellow nature of the conservative and liberal prioritizing of the

Reclaiming Imagination

conservatives, liberals can rely too optimistically on an objective approach to the Bible's content (i.e., attempts to reconstruct the history behind the Gospels or to draw out of the text a universal moral message). Kierkegaard's emphasis on imaginative engagement with the biblical text suggests a prophetic movement away from the bibliolatry and doctrinal propositionalism of conservative evangelicalism and the historicism/moralism of liberalism, and toward a spiritually transformational, imaginative appropriation of the biblical text. As we will show, Kierkegaard's own interpretations and use of Scripture provide a model of employing the imagination to enter a narrative world originally created by the biblical authors, under the inspiration of the Spirit, but continually made fresh by the Spirit's active engagement with readers and hearers.

THE MODERN PROBLEM: THE DIMINISHED IMAGINATION

Garrett Green, in *Theology, Hermeneutics and Imagination*, suggests that the crisis of modernity stemmed from its rejection of a positive function for the imagination in religion. He shows how, underneath the deconstructionist moves of Nietzsche, Heidegger, and Derrida, one can hear the voice of Ludwig Feuerbach, the "pure modernist." For Feuerbach, religion is constructed by human beings as they extrapolate their God-images upon a curtain of myth, symbol, and ritual; the religious imagination is therefore a false consciousness. The modernist project included the deconstruction of the religious imagination in order to arrive at pure, "objective" truth. Consider these titles of key Enlightenment philosophers: *The Reasonableness of Christianity* (John Locke) and *Religion within the Limits of Reason Alone* (Immanuel Kant). Enlightenment figures advocated the maturation of religion beyond the "childhood" of mythology and the trappings of tradition into the rational maturity of intellectual freedom: Kant's mantra, *sapere aude!* ("Dare to know!"), while encouraging a certain sort of imagination, excluded the concreteness of the religious in the sacred texts of divine revelation. Green suggests that at the heart of modernism lies a rejection of a positive role for the religious imagination. He states, "Theologians in the age of modernity, now rapidly approaching its end, have resisted the suggestion that Christian faith is a mode of imagination."[3]

"objectivity" of the text, see Green, *Theology, Hermeneutics, and Imagination*.

3. Green, *Theology, Hermeneutics, and Imagination*, 205.

In this way, at least, postmodernism can be thought of as the flip side of modernity in that it attempts reclamation of the imagination. Green suggests that postmodernism can fall into another ditch, in which *everything* is understood to be the product of human imagination; creative, finite constructions of "reality" are all we have.[4] Rather than idolize rationality for its supposed ability to articulate the givenness of reality (modernity), postmodernism idolizes the imagination for its ability to *construct* "reality." But if all knowledge is constructed, how can anyone (individuals, communities, denominations, etc.) adjudicate between imaginative constructions? This is a common critique of the postmodern, supposedly "relativist," condition. Green suggests, with more sympathy for a postmodernist than a modernist approach, that a way forward for Christian believers is via the intentional recovery of the "hermeneutic imperative." That is, while the postmodern situation entails complex and even troubling questions regarding the adjudication of interpretations and the construction of "reality," the implication of the hermeneutical imperative is that postmodern Christians have an opportunity to tap into the rich resources of their own tradition, including the narrative, poetry, and parables of Scripture, and reinterpret those traditions in contemporary contexts.

For Green, the diversity of the Bible's forms and content validate the divinely sanctioned function of human imagination. As he states, "God has chosen to reveal himself not in transparent doctrines appealing to reason but in opaque symbols and narratives that appeal to the imagination."[5] The fact that God has chosen to reveal himself (in part) through the diversity of the Bible's textual forms suggests that human interpretation—and imagination—is required.[6] This would seem obvious, except for the persistence of a positivist hermeneutic that assumes, at some level, that the meaning (often understood as the *single* meaning) of biblical texts can be objectively—and even exhaustively—interpreted by a simple application of interpretive procedures. This sensibility has been confirmed to me anecdotally in class discussions with conservative evangelical students. Students occasionally insist that a particular biblical text "does not need to be interpreted, because *the* meaning is self-evident."

Another way of putting the issue is to say that, under the rubric of modernist hermeneutics, interpreting the text faithfully often involves the

4. Ibid., 143–66.
5. Ibid., 182.
6. Ibid., 172.

basic use of a standard methodology (e.g., grammatical-historical criticism, form criticism, source criticism, etc.). Proper use of the methodology ensures a perfectly accurate, if not exhaustive, interpretation. This emphasis on method neglects the subjectivity of the interpreter. In postliberal and in postmodern hermeneutics, attention is given to the interpreter as much as to the method (and content) of interpretation. Stanley Hauerwas, for example, critiques both fundamentalists and liberals for wanting "to make Christianity available to the person of common sense without moral transformation."[7] To interpret is to involve oneself, as an interpreter, in the text. To be involved means that one's personhood, one's subjectivity, at least partly determines the meaning(s).

The "hermeneutic imperative" suggests that, because meaning is indefinite and precludes finality, given the finitude and situatedness of interpreters, the imagination plays a key role in the Christian life. This runs against "dead literalism" and requires that the Word be *heard* in fresh, contextually relevant, and existentially probing ways. For Green, "the Bible appeals not to the theoretical faculties directly but to the imagination."[8]

Appreciating the positive role of the imagination in reading and interpreting Scripture as well as in doing theology creates a positive inspiration for the constructive theological task, including projects such as feminist and liberation theologies (although, ironically, Green is highly critical of these projects).[9] When the role of imagination is prioritized, the dynamics of contemporary context are set in motion in connection with a community's reading of and interaction around Scripture. As readers seek after justice and righteousness in their contexts, they can attend freshly to Scripture's own representation of these themes. The burgeoning discourse of *theological interpretation* in evangelical theology suggests a widening appreciation for the conscious use of a discerning imagination in biblical interpretation, which transcends mere objectivity.[10]

For Green, when the modernist epistemology project began to crumble, the task of theology shifted to recovering a "unity of imagination and reality, and to begin to utilize the imagination in connection with the Bible

---

7. Hauerwas, *Unleashing the Scripture*, 35–36.

8. Green, *Theology, Hermeneutics, and Imagination*, 178.

9. Ibid., 202–3.

10. For two recent examples, see Treier, *Introducing Theological Interpretation*, and Billings, *The Word of God for the People of God*.

and in the practice of theology in context."[11] Green's diagnosis of the loss of the imagination in modernity is on target; furthermore, his proposal for the revitalization of the imagination in postmodernity runs parallel to the ethos and project of the emergent church. Once again, Kierkegaard offers much insight in regard to a positive function for the imagination in Christian faith and practice.

KIERKEGAARD, THE IMAGINATION, AND THE IMITATION OF CHRIST

"Imagination is what providence uses to take [people] captive in actuality [*Virkeligheden*], in order to get them far enough out, or within, or down into actuality. And when imagination has helped them get as far out as they should be—then actuality genuinely begins."[12]

Kierkegaard is recognized among the great philosophers and religious thinkers of Western thought for his uniquely creative intellect. He not only extolled the virtues of the imagination, but he also exercised his own imaginative abilities in his writing. As we have noted, Kierkegaard created an impressive cast of pseudonyms as "authors" of his books and developed a highly creative, nuanced, and complex corpus of texts. He employed parable, poetry, humor, satire, irony, devotional reflection, as well as highly intricate didactic material among his varied use of genre. While the point of his writing was, by and large, quite serious (to "reintroduce New Testament Christianity into Christendom"), he apparently had a good bit of fun in the process. Since Kierkegaard so clearly appreciated the positive function of the imagination, he can be seen (once again) as a bridge figure between modernism and postmodernism. Writing at the height of modernity, Kierkegaard's religious philosophy both employed and explicitly recognized the power of the imagination in the formulation of an authentic religious consciousness and in the service of genuine, vibrant religious experience.

This discussion of the role of the imagination takes us back to chapter 1, where we examined Kierkegaard's understanding of the development of the self. We noted there that, for Kierkegaard, the self is a synthesis of eternity and temporality, of necessity and possibility, of finitude and

---

11. Green, *Theology, Hermeneutics, and Imagination*, 205.
12. *JP* 2, 1832.

infinitude. This dialectic of the self implies that rigorous tensions emerge as the self continues to develop as a unified person "before God." An improperly related self will be drawn by the pull of possibility such that she becomes lost in the sphere of the "fantastic" (e.g., speculation);[13] or she will be grounded in the mundane concretion of actuality such that the burden of despair squelches her freedom to exist as a self. For Kierkegaard, "the philistine-bourgeois mentality," or the spiritlessness, of modernity "lacks possibility."[14] On the other hand, to be "spirit" is to be motivated by the gift of possibility and potentiality—particularly by the belief that (for God) all things are possible: "Only he whose being has been so shaken that he has become spirit by understanding that everything is possible, only he has anything to do with God."[15]

That all things are possible for God is manifest in the fact that the God-man, the absolute paradox and contradiction beyond human thought, could exist as a single individual within finitude and temporality. The incarnation inspires confidence in God's absolute love and power (his willingness to use his power *against* himself) and stirs hope in the human heart. It makes sense, then, that the paradox of the God-man would stand, for Kierkegaard, as the image that most powerfully evokes the passion of possibility within human beings by fervently stirring the religious imagination. To become contemporary with Christ is to have one's imagination awakened to the fullest degree, but without losing oneself to the "fantastical"; to put it bluntly, one gains one's "soul" without losing one's mind.

The imitation of Christ is central to Kierkegaard's deconstruction of modernist ideologies. Because the gospel involves the narrative of Jesus Christ, the recipient of the gospel is confronted with a living person, the God-man. As Kierkegaard says, "truth is a being . . . a life,"[16] and "I only know the truth when it becomes a life in me."[17] The gospel presents the possibility for new relationships between God and humanity, which, though fractured, can be restored by God's grace in Christ existentially appropriated by the single individual. But this appropriation involves an

---

13. The "intoxicating" draw of possibility, if unchecked by reality, could lead one into the realm of the fantastic, and thus to the loss of the authentic self. *EO1*, 41.

14. *SUD*, 41.

15. *SUD*, 40.

16. *JFY*, 198–99.

17. *PC*, 201.

active following of Christ in obedience. As Kierkegaard puts it, "imitation must be affirmed to press toward humility. This, quite simply, is how it is done. Everyone must be measured by the prototype, by the ideal."[18]

The Bible teaches people *about* Christ; but it simultaneously (and more importantly) commands people to *follow* the Christ of which it speaks. It does so by presenting a powerful portrait of a loving Savior who calls out to humanity: "Come to me, all you who are weary and burdened, and I will give you rest" (Matt 11:28).

To hear the story of the God-man is simultaneously to be confronted with the possibility—at once alluring and repulsive—to follow Christ by becoming contemporary with him. The narratives of Jesus invite love, worship, and obedience. To learn *about* Jesus and believe in him in a cognitive or intellectual sense is not yet to fully *understand* him in a spiritual and experiential sense. Such understanding is reserved for the one who has faith *in* Jesus. Nonetheless, Kierkegaard seemed to fully acknowledge that to experience Christ necessitates some knowledge about him. Where do we get this knowledge except from the Bible? Engagement with Scripture is, then, an essential component of the imitation of Christ. But to engage with Scripture dynamically involves the active development of the religious imagination. Following Christ is an imaginative and interpretive (and therefore hermeneutical) venture.

APPROPRIATION, IMAGINATION, AND BIBLICAL INTERPRETATION

For Kierkegaard, the appropriation of the truth of Christianity requires an ongoing development of the imagination. The meaning of Scripture is not single, static, and universal, but a product of a dynamic interplay between author, text, and reader as the reader (or hearer) appropriates the text, making it *his or her own*—with the help of the Spirit. Kierkegaard sheds light

---

18. *JFY*, 188. For Kierkegaard, only through the presentation of the New Testament ideal of the imitation of Christ could Christianity be reintroduced into Christendom: "If Christianity is to be reintroduced into Christendom, it must again be proclaimed unconditionally as imitation, as law, so Christianity does not become the conjunctive (which sanctifies all our cherished relationships and our earthly fortune and striving) but the disjunctive: to let go of everything, to hate one's father and mother and oneself" (*JP* 1, 401). The Danish word for imitation, *efterføgelse*, suggests "following" rather than "copying." This rendering more accurately describes Kierkegaard's concept than does the English connotation of "facsimile," in which one simply copies the object of one's imitation.

on this concept in his preface to one of his *Three Discourses on Imagined Occasions*. There he says that his book

> seeks that single individual whom I with joy and gratitude call *my* reader, or it does not even seek him. Unaware of the time and the hour, it quietly waits for that right reader to come like the bridegroom and to bring the occasion along with him. Let each do a share—the reader therefore more. The meaning lies in the appropriation. Hence the *book's* joyous *giving of itself*. Here there are no worldly "mine" and "thine" that separate and prohibit appropriating what is the neighbor's . . . and the appropriation is the *reader's* even greater, is his triumphant *giving of himself*.[19]

The reader is an active participant in the production of meaning—certainly in the production of existentially and religiously significant meaning.[20] In his unpublished *Lectures on Communication*, Kierkegaard, discussing the relation between the communicator and the receiver of the communication, said, "'receiver' is an active word . . . we have no passive word [for this concept]."[21] This fits well with Kierkegaard's emphasis on the responsibility of the reader of his own writings, whom he affectionately called "that single reader." In his preface to the *Three Discourses* of 1844, Kierkegaard said his book seeks the reader who "gives an opportunity to what is said, brings the cold thoughts into flame again, transforms the discourse into a conversation."[22] In another reflection on his discourses, he encouraged his reader to "think about the occasion [the reader's life situation] very vividly" and to imagine as if the discourse "were speaking directly to you." This active reading is what Kierkegaard calls the reader's "self-activity."[23]

---

19. *TDIO*, 5.

20. Kierkegaard's emphasis on subjective appropriation—and the responsibility of the reader in actualizing meaning—is suggestive of what in postmodern literary theory is known as "reader-response" hermeneutics. However, it is more likely that Kierkegaard is advocating a "fusion of horizons," in the same vein as Hans-Georg Gadamer's suggestion in *Truth and Method*. We will look deeper into Gadamer subsequently in this chapter. The key here is that Kierkegaard understands meaning to be the result of a communicative event, which occurs in the "dialogue" between reader and text (and in an implied but distant sense, the author also). This does not mean that meaning is unconstrained or arbitrary.

21. *JP* 1, 650.

22. *EUD*, 231.

23. *UDVS*, 123.

Emerging Prophet

In the preface to his *Three Upbuilding Discourses*, Kierkegaard requests a favor of his readers: that they read his work aloud. The reader's voice will break "the spell on the letters" and summon forth what the "mute letters have on their lips."[24] The reader has the power to "rescue" the author's otherwise entrapped, silent words and make them come alive in the context of his or her concrete actuality. This highlights the conversational, event-nature of appropriation and the dynamic nature of meaning: the words are *for me* (the reader) and they come alive in my engagement with them.

Anthony Thiselton resonates with Kierkegaard when he suggests, "it is in the *application* of a piece of language in which meaning and understanding, as a communicative act or process, reside; not in some second-level category distanced and demoted into mere connotation or resonance by the term 'significance' in contrast to meaning."[25] The meaning/significance dichotomy cannot be countenanced in an existentially focused hermeneutic. Nonetheless, in Christian theology, the role of the divine author in textual communication cannot be neglected either.[26]

There is more to interpretation, liturgy, worship, preaching, and theology than *human* imagination and *human* agency. For Kierkegaard, *God* plays an integral role in creating understanding in the reader/hearer, both in their inspiration and in their illumination of the reader. In Kierkegaard's hermeneutic, responsibility also lies with the reader, but part of that includes recognizing Scripture's divine origin, religious authority, and transformational purpose. Yet, God does not leave the willing reader "alone." Kierkegaard ended his *Two Upbuilding Discourses* of 1843 with a prayer for the "Father of lights" to provide an "understanding of the words" and "heal the misunderstanding heart so that it understands

---

24. *EUD*, 53.

25. Thiselton, "'Behind' and 'In Front of' the Text," 104. For a more explicitly postmodern framing of hermeneutics, see Adam, "Integral and Differential Hermeneutics." He advocates a "differential hermeneutic" approach that allows for legitimate interpretive differences while retaining boundaries of "faithful" interpretation.

26. Thiselton writes, "The whole communicative act is not completed by the 'sender' alone. Textual actualization entails author or personal sources, code, content, contact, context and reception, appropriation, application or understanding on the part of implied readers, addressees or actual readers. In Christian theology, the definitive givenness of Scripture remains both authoritative and potential in meaning on the ground that the same Holy Spirit who inspired the agents who wrote will also inspire the prophets, teachers, congregations and seekers who read" ("'Behind' and 'In Front of' the Text," 107–8).

the words . . ."²⁷ In *For Self-Examination,* he suggested that God, "the Infinitely Sublime One," is "the one who with more than human—indeed, with divine—patience sits and spells out the Word with the single individual so that he may understand it aright"; furthermore, God "helps him when he strive to act according to it . . ."²⁸

For Kierkegaard the divine presence can be experienced in our attempts to read, understand, and obey the words of Scripture in the concrete actuality and particularities of life. The reality of the presence of the Spirit in the process of understanding and appropriating Scripture is a welcome encouragement to the one who strives to make its words her or his own. It is a reminder of the grace of God dispensed in the world and is another aspect of God's communicating presence in the midst of a fallen and finite existence.

"Imaginative Identification" and the Plenitude of Meaning

Kierkegaard's understanding of and approach to biblical interpretation shows that he viewed interpretation as neither completely indeterminate nor completely determinate. Furthermore, he viewed language as neither univocal (a one-to-one correspondence between a word as "sign" and an object as the thing "signified") nor equivocal (words are arbitrary signs that do not correspond ontologically with the "reality" or object they purport to reflect). Rather, his understanding of how language works likely stands somewhere between those two poles. In consequence, as Timothy Polk suggests, religious appropriation of Scripture's meaning "requires readers' creative and personal engagement for its completion . . ."²⁹

Kierkegaard's approach to this "creative and personal engagement" was through highlighting the activity of the imagination. In an influential survey of Kierkegaard's use of the Bible, Paul Minear and Paul Morimoto suggested that Kierkegaard practiced a "silent absorption" of the text, in which he (or his pseudonym) would retreat to a secret place and imaginatively "become" Job or Abraham, so that he could "slip more fully out of his own and into the costume of the Biblical author."³⁰ Kierkegaard's use of

---

27. *EUD,* 48.
28. *FSE,* 13–14.
29. Polk, *Biblical Kierkegaard,* 71.
30. Minear and Morimoto, *Kierkegaard and the Bible,* 10. On the imitation of Abraham, see *Fear and Trembling.* On the imitation of Job, see *Repetition.* Both texts are

James' metaphor (the mirror of the word, from James 1:22–25) in *For Self-Examination* commends this interpretive method of entering into the world of the text such that the text becomes more than an object of knowledge. It functions as a "mirror" through which the reader acquires self-perception and by which one experiences spiritual transformation. Hermeneutics is linked with subjectivity (and passion) in the quest for knowledge and existential authenticity.[31]

Janet Fishburn has called Kierkegaard's approach the "principle of imaginative identification."[32] Within broad constraints, the meaning of a text changes depending on the reader's actual situation and how the text—or God *through* the text—speaks to the reader. From the same text, one can preach both "rigor" and "mildness."[33] Legitimate meanings could be derived from multiple perspectives, depending on the differing situations of the readers.[34] The richness of Scripture's potential meaning affords readers in all spheres of existence opportunity to reflect on their lives, to be challenged by the text, and to be transformed by submitting to the truth that the text presents—all through the use of imaginative identification. The key determinant of a true understanding depends upon whether the reader understands that the words are *addressed* to him or her. Kierkegaard's use of

---

included in *FT*.

31. Perhaps no section of Kierkegaard's writings better illustrates his conviction regarding the essential importance of the imagination in biblical interpretation than his examination of the parable of the Good Samaritan. In his exposition, no single, universal meaning (e.g., "we should all be good neighbors to those in need") is derived from the story. Rather, the reader's task is to identify with whichever character in the story best approximates his or her actual situation. Kierkegaard expands beyond what is given in the narrative (priest, Levite, Samaritan), creating characters not present in the gospel account, including a "practical man" and "someone in deep thought, thinking about nothing," whose preoccupations caused him to ignore the wounded man lying on the road (*FSE*, 40–41).

32. Fishburn, "Søren Kierkegaard, Exegete," 229–45. Fishburn suggests that Kierkegaard's hermeneutical approach reflects a "principle of imitation through imaginative identification." She summarizes Kierkegaard's treatment of Scripture well: "In response to the search for the factually true or historically probable elements in the Bible that influenced the interpretation of his day, Kierkegaard persisted in seeking the truth in Scripture through imaginative and total immersion in its content." Ibid., 229.

33. *WL*, 347.

34. In *Practice in Christianity*, Kierkegaard writes, "But to confirm this we shall not fail to cite the person who not only as the author of these words is the best interpreter of his own words but by his divine authority calls for silence and cuts off all further interpretation if it does not lead to the same interpretation: the Apostle John" (*PC*, 259).

the New Testament reveals sensitivity to a plenitude of meaning. Nonetheless, he respected the "sacred text" and the responsibility of the interpreter to adequately interpret the meaning of a biblical text (respecting the divine author of the text) for one's existential situation.[35] Biblical interpretation was not an "anything goes" affair: among other things, Kierkegaard's consistently orthodox Christology would suggest otherwise.

The plenitude of meaning is a consequence of the responsibility of the individual interpreter to engage the text (and through it, God). Interpretation of Scripture is no light matter. In an ominous journal reflection, Kierkegaard wrote:

> He gives men [sic] a holy book which contains his will but contains no middle terms in relation to the ideal—and then he leaves it up to each one how he is going to understand it. He is not to be heard from, keeps perfectly quiet, testing the single individual, for it actually seems to be left completely up to us how we are to understand Scripture. But it goes without saying—judgment is coming.[36]

The individual bears a great responsibility in interpreting Scripture: "judgment is coming." God gives a revelation, which expresses the ideal for what it means to follow in the way of Jesus, but he gives "no middle terms" in relation to it. The reader is left to ask how he or she, *in concreto*, is supposed to live out the ideal of the New Testament in his or her own life.[37] With freedom comes responsibility, and with responsibility the possibility, in this case, of interpreting and therefore of appropriating a text in the context of actual life in a manner that neither attains the New Testament's ideal nor matches the individual's life situation. Hermeneutics requires a struggle of the single individual, "before God," as he or she reads and appropriates the New Testament. Kierkegaard called this existentially earnest interpretation "primitive" reading. An adequate interpretation

35. Ibid.
36. *JP* 3, 2882.
37. David Law notes a lack of concrete, detailed direction in Kierkegaard's *For Self-Examination* regarding what discipleship should look like in the nineteenth century. He states, "We are told we must die away to the world, but it is left unclear what this entails in the situations, problems, and crises which we encounter on a daily basis in our lives in the world." See Law's "Cheap Grace and the Cost of Discipleship in Kierkegaard's *For Self-Examination*," 135–36. I would argue, however, that Kierkegaard's "abstract" (an interesting word to apply to Kierkegaard in any sense!) presentation of discipleship is intentional, cohering as it does with his view of each individual reader's "primitive" responsibility to interpret the text in accordance with God's leading in his or her actual, *concrete* situation.

reveals a deep connection between the world of the text and one's own actual situation. We might call this a fit between the *words* and the *world* (though in a particular way, the *world* of the reader). When this connection occurs, the reader may be comforted (if he or she is in need of comfort), or he or she may be convicted (if he or she is in need of correction). When the fit is right, the interpretation rings true—and is appropriated. In Kierkegaard's perspective, the interpretive space for individual, contextual appropriation fits God's intention for biblical revelation. God desires that every person "interpret it each according to his own wisdom . . ."[38] The act of biblical interpretation is implicated in Kierkegaard's emphasis on the *primitivity* of the God-relationship—every person is ultimately responsible "before God" for their orientation to the eternal.[39]

This notion of primitive reading may seem to run against many contemporary discussions in philosophical and biblical hermeneutics—particularly those empathetic with postmodernity. Is interpretation, on Kierkegaard's account, relegated to the sphere of the merely private—the individualistic? Is that not modernism? Is the role of the community, and of tradition, in interpretation marginalized or ruled out altogether? Furthermore, does this approach render interpretation immune from any public criterion or criticism?[40] While we should not forget the postmodern reminder of the communal construction of meaning, Kierkegaard pushes

---

38. *JP* 3, 2807. A relational element underscores all that he says about the reader and the New Testament. The New Testament is a gift of God to the single individual and is given so that the reader might grow in his or her relational knowledge of God. Furthermore, God, through the action of the Spirit, plays a determinative role in guiding the reader to understand what *he or she needs to understand* in order to be edified in the God-relationship.

39. Every human being, Kierkegaard said, is "intended and outfitted for" a primitive relationship to God, in which "he stands alone, alone, alone with God" (*JP* 3, 2907). As Howard and Edna Hong explain, the Danish *primitivt* means "an individual's freshness and authenticity in thinking, feeling, acting, and responding. It designates the opposite of habit, external conformity, and aping" (*PF*, 317).

40. Timothy Polk, in *The Biblical Kierkegaard*, argues that Kierkegaard's hermeneutics can be interpreted in the same vein as "postliberal" hermeneutics (represented by George Lindbeck and Hans Frei)—despite Kierkegaard's repeated concerns with subjectivity and the "single individual." In a review of Polk's book, Amy Laurel Hall suggested that Polk's thesis might be a case of special pleading. Nonetheless, she affirmed that Kierkegaard's emphasis on the individual's responsibility in interpretation might be positively corrected by a turn to the concerns of postliberal theology for the role of community in interpretation.

Reclaiming Imagination

us to think of the *appropriation* of religious truth and engagement with Scripture as ultimately each individual's responsibility *before God*.

Furthermore, Kierkegaard's understanding of subjectivity includes a social, communal dynamic in the formation of the religious imagination. Nonetheless, he commends to the "single individual" the role of the imagination in articulating the meaning of the Bible and in appropriating that to the Christian life. Kierkegaard's hermeneutic is dynamic, not static: the *meaning lies in the appropriation;* existentially significant meaning is the consequence of the contact between reader, text, and the divine presence. Kierkegaard's respect for the Bible's divine authority and its christological center is held in a positive tension with the concern for the imaginative, personal (and contextual) appropriation of Scripture. Two notions central to Kierkegaard's thought about biblical interpretation prevent his hermeneutic from static ossification: the truth of subjectivity and his view that Christianity is an existence-communication. The Bible, then, as God's medium of communication, is a dynamic instrument of revelation through which God exerts his loving authority in communicating truth and meaning—teaching everything about "the divine" to humanity "from the beginning," and inviting the reader to respond to God's voice.[41]

Kierkegaard's emphasis on individual subjectivity can stand to be corrected—or supplemented—by the insights of postmodern thought regarding the influence of community on interpretation, belief, and theology. But Kierkegaard's understanding of the Bible as a dynamic instrument of divine revelation that evokes an imaginative response is right on target with the ethos of emergent Christianity and is an important corrective to static, objective (modernist) hermeneutics of Scripture. In what follows, I engage hermeneutics in a "postmodern key," as we explore the individual and communal imagination in interpreting the Bible.

POSTMODERNITY, HERMENEUTICS, AND IMAGINATION

"Interpretation is not the reiteration of the text. It is rather the movement of the text beyond itself in fresh ways, often ways never offered until this moment of utterance."[42]

---

41. *EUD*, 327.
42. Brueggemann, *Book that Breathes New Life*, 28.

Like Kierkegaard, emergent Christians recognize that the meaning of a text transcends the author's and original reader's historical setting (the "original meaning") and is "added to" by the reader—and community—who engages it. Hans-Georg Gadamer, leading light of philosophical hermeneutics, noted: "Not just occasionally but always, the meaning of a text goes beyond its author. That is why understanding is not merely a reproductive but always a productive activity as well."[43] Hermeneutics requires active participation in the creation of meaning. It may be worth noting that, while it seems jarring to conservative evangelical ears, the reality is that we already do this (and have for over two thousand years). It is difficult to deny that the established use of terms like *trinitas* ("Trinity") and *homoousios* ("of the same substance") as interpretive keys to understanding the Bible are—at least in part—consequences of contextually located, passionate, issue-specific, communal engagements with the meaning of biblical texts. This is not to question their truth and their ongoing significance as theological concepts; however, it is to point out that meanings emerge in a dialogical response to a text and to contemporary concerns raised by a text in new situations; meanings transcend the historical, empirical author's original intent. The question is whether readers are engaging texts with seriousness, passion, and faithfulness. In other words, readers ought to engage the biblical text with one eye on the weight of historical tradition as theological guide (and to what patristic theologians called the "rule of faith") and another eye on the contemporary setting, attending to what God might be calling them toward in the present. Might it be that biblical interpretation has a *missional* purpose?

For Brueggemann, when we apply a "cold, reiterative objectivity" to Scripture, we discover that this objective approach lacks "missional energy or moral force."[44] An intentionally imaginative engagement with Scripture invites passion, obedience, and love (resulting in a missional response to the text). Because imaginative reading involves "the high practice of subjective extrapolations," it also generates anxiety, because it rules out epistemic certainty. As the activity of human, creative subjectivity, the hermeneutical imagination can claim "only the tentativeness of our best extrapolations."[45] Nonetheless, while the application of the religious imagination (the active en-

---

43. Gadamer, *Truth and Method*, 296, cited in Westphal, *Whose Community? Which Interpretation?*, 62.

44. Brueggemann, *Book that Breathes New Life*, 29.

45. Ibid., 30.

ergizing of the self in relation to the text) differs from mere observation or intellectual comprehension, the imagination is the "vehicle for interpretation."[46]

What if in denigrating or relegating a constructive role of the imagination we have cut off our most vital source for witness and mission? God invites us to engage Scripture not just for its original meaning, but also with a focus on the appropriation of its words to a new context—God calls us to wrestle anew with the text. What is the Spirit saying to the churches as they read, preach, proclaim, and interact around this text? Mere observation can be limiting, but the active imagination faithfully and passionately engaged with the text can be life-giving—and is that not what Jesus desires for us (John 10:10)?

Emergent pastors Conder and Rhodes reflect Brueggemann's influence on their articulation of the importance of the imagination in engaging Scripture. In *Free for All: Rediscovering the Bible in Community,* they note the same connection between subjectivity/imagination and missional vitality that we find in Brueggemann. They acknowledge the influence of postmodernity on the way that we read Scripture and suggest that the shift is something to be embraced rather than to be feared. They suggest that within a postmodern framework, the Bible is freed to be the "living, active Word of God rather than an abstract, impersonal message" and is embodied in a "mutually dependent worship community."[47] The imagination is an essential skill of an earnest reader of the Bible. Conversely, the lack of imagination helps explain what they call the church's "flat-earth moments." Where the church has rigidly stood fast on a received literalistic interpretation of the text, the church has done damage to its mission. A good example would be the unwillingness of many Christians today to rethink the meaning of Genesis 1–3 in light of contemporary scientific understandings of the universe's (and humanity's) origins. The fundamentalist interpretation prevents a more theologically interesting and more missional engagement with the text. Conder and Rhodes suggest that the unwillingness to challenge such received interpretations shows a lack of skill, artistry, and creativity in hermeneutical and theological imagination. What the church needs more of, they say (along with solid exegesis and earnest prayer), are some "bold expenditures of imagination," which could catalyze the church for a freshly empowered mission in our increasingly post-Christian, postmodern context.[48]

46. Ibid., 29.
47. Conder and Rhodes, *Free for All*, 54–55.
48. Ibid., 234.

It should be noted, however, that for Brueggemann, the active (and subjective) use of the imagination in interpretation and theology should be sharply distinguished from ideology, which he describes as the "self-deceiving practice of taking a part for the whole, of taking 'my truth' for *the* truth, of running truth through a prism of the particular and palming off the particular as a universal."[49] The imagination involves, no doubt, the exercise of human subjectivity in relation to textual interpretation; therefore, the results are human "constructions," in a sense. But they are not ideological insofar as the ones practicing the hermeneutical imagination resist the temptation to close the interpretive process too hastily. For Brueggemann, faithful engagement with the text is to be always open, through critical reflection, to fresh readings and rereadings; deconstruction and reconstruction are always happening.[50]

From Individual Autonomy to Community Answerability

The recovery of an intentionally constructive role for the imagination in biblical interpretation and theology is an essential element of emergent Christianity—and was exemplified by Kierkegaard's interpretation of the Bible. Kierkegaard pressed both for individual responsibility and creative flexibility in engaging the Scripture and thinking theologically. But a question arises: Does this emphasis on subjectivity and imagination necessarily lead to relativism—even hermeneutical anarchy? Do we find ourselves unable to speak of meaning and of truth outside of one's personal response? Does it not amount to a *de facto* "death of the author," for which postmodernism is so feared?

Westphal offers some help here. He proposes a way beyond the "vertigo of [hermeneutical] relativity," or the anxieties that come with the admission that absolute, determinate meaning is neither desirable nor possible. Are readers simply creating meaning out of thin air, with no regard to textual boundaries?[51] For Christians who emphasize Scripture as

---

49. Ibid., 30.

50. Ibid., 131–40

51. Westphal defines it thus: "Since there are many interpreters and traditions, there will be a 'veritable plethora' of interpretations, each relative to a different perspective. The text will be dissolved or dispersed at the cost of its identity. It will mean everything and therefore nothing." He refers to modernist/Romanticist philosopher of hermeneutics Dilthey's question: "But where are the means to overcome the anarchy of opinions that threaten to befall us?" *Whose Community? Which Interpretation?*, 45–46.

Reclaiming Imagination

the authoritative text for church practices, liturgy, ethics, discipleship, and theology, the "vertigo of relativity" can be especially disorienting. Westphal insists that Christians can protect themselves against hermeneutic relativism without recourse to the tools of modernist (fundamentalist) objectivism.[52] Resources are available within the postmodern turn to community.

Postmodern hermeneutics shifts the burden from the autonomy of the text and from the autonomy of the individual interpreter to a dialogical, communal understanding of meaning. In this approach, meaning is created in the event of reading or hearing the text. Meanings are coproduced by the author and the reader (and the reading community) as a "product of their interaction." They each contribute to the "determinacy of meaning without requiring that it [the text's meaning] be absolutely determinate."[53] In this approach, there are hermeneutical boundaries; a text cannot legitimately mean *anything*. The range of legitimate meanings is constrained by the responsible interaction between readers, the author, and the text (a product of authorial intention—or, in Kevin Vanhoozer's words, what an author was "attending to in tending to his words").[54] Nonetheless, the actual event of interpretation sanctions hermeneutical flexibility, allowing for variations of meaning depending on the reader's context and existential situation.[55] It allows, in other words, for the subjective appropriation of truth.

This dialectic includes both the community and the individual in the determination of textual meaning. For Walter Brueggemann, the function of the imagination is tied to the role of community in interpretation. In *Texts Under Negotiation*, he suggests that interpreters have a "zone of imagination" that persists between the "input of the text" and the "outcome of attitude, belief, or behavior." In other words, there is a good bit of "material" within the experience of the interpreter that must be accounted for; this material is both inevitable and legitimate in the interpretive process. The

---

52. Ibid., 46.

53. Ibid., 54.

54. Vanhoozer, *Is There a Meaning in This Text?*, 262.

55. Westphal writes, "Might not the meaning(s) of a text be coproduced by author and reader, the product of their interaction? Might not each contribute to the determinacy of meaning without requiring that it be absolutely determinate? If the author has a legitimate role, without needing to be an autocrat, then the text cannot mean just anything that any reader takes it to mean. There will be boundaries, as Hirsch requires. But if the reader also plays a role, these boundaries will be sufficiently generous to allow that a given text might legitimately mean somewhat different things to different people in different circumstances." *Whose Community? Which Interpretation?*, 54.

zone of imagination, Brueggemann asserts, is "in part shaped by the community." At the same time, it is a "protected place of intimacy and interiority that I keep for my very self."[56] The zone of imagination is dynamically shaped by an ongoing dialectic of community and personal subjectivity.

Brueggemann's dialectic is a crucial one to sustain for Christians in postmodernity. Individual subjectivities are not sealed off from other subjectivities. Human beings are inextricably relational; even if we attempt isolation, others impact us. Interpretation involves more than just a "fusion of horizons" (Gadamer) of the individual reader and author/text; the reader's horizon includes also his or her community of readers—the interpretive traditions in which he or she was (and is being) formed. The role of the community serves to facilitate an ongoing dialogue, with corrections, amendments, confirmations, etc., regarding what texts can and should mean. Interaction within communities and across communities is vital to preserving and fertilizing the "answerability" that such communities provide.[57] Churches explicitly identified with emergent Christianity are known for promoting and instilling within their communal lives the active practice of dialogical interpretation. Scripture does not mean simply what the pastor (or a given theologian) declares it to mean; Scripture *means* as local or otherwise connected communities (i.e., denominations) engage passionately and faithfully with the text in light of how the Spirit is speaking through it to them—in their contexts.

Imagination, Community, and Liturgy

While we have been focusing on the active use of the imagination in the interpretation of Scripture, discussion of the imagination could extend further. The entire liturgical experience invites much fertile discussion as to the role for an active, religious imagination. Emergent philosopher Peter Rollins, in an essay reflecting on the emerging church movement, suggests that emergent Christians are drawn to imaginative liturgical practices, such as transformation art, which "can be described as an immersive art form that invites people to engage in a theatrical, ritualistic performance whereby they enact the death of God (as *deus ex machina*) and the resurrection of

---

56. Brueggemann, *Texts Under Negotiation*, 62.

57. Westphal suggests that postmodern hermeneutics shifts the burden from the autonomy of the text (premodern) and from the autonomy of the individual interpreter (modern) to the *answerability* of the interpreting community.

Reclaiming Imagination

God (as one who dwells among us) with the purpose of reconfiguring one's social existence."[58] The practice of transformance art, he says, arises out of a desire to transform one's social space, which sometimes necessitates "convincing the architecture," by inhabiting spaces that more fully reflect and "embody commitments to the world, to humility, doubt, and complexity . . . helping us to become what we already believe."[59] Emergent Christianity validates the creative application of the imagination to all arenas of life, including worship, liturgy, engagement with Scripture, and theology. Emergent leaders are tapping into the current burgeoning recognition of creativity as one of the most valuable resources of our society. In this technological and creative era, the church also desires to link up with the fresh burst of creativity in our culture. Tim Keel, writing of the recognition within the emergent church of the significance of the imagination, notes:

> My purpose in writing these things is not to denigrate facts, data, or cognition, but to say that in the world we live in now, facts alone are not adequate. They never were. And the artists, poets, prophets, contemplatives, and mystics among us have been witnessing to this from the margins for a long time. Artists and poets and others in our midst are in tune with the collective, intuitive, and spiritual. They have honored their senses and intuitive capacities in a way that allows for a radical engagement with the environment, with reality, to reflect, respond, and create something that is true and vital and defining. They are leading us somewhere.[60]

The church, Keel suggests, must be attentive to this cultural shift and not lose the opportunity to integrate creativity and imagination into its own practices and structures. The church is in danger of "missing this fundamental shift."[61]

A danger lurks in the excitement about the imagination, whether applied to biblical interpretation and theology or to other practices within the church and Christian life. A recovery of the role of the imagination in religion should not cause an undue exaltation of the poet, the artist, or the musician (or even of the imaginative biblical interpreter or theologian!) over other vocations represented in the church.[62] Indeed, this would be,

---

58. Rollins, "Transformance Art," 98.
59. Ibid., 101.
60. Keel, "Leading from the Margins," 228–29.
61. Ibid., 229.
62. Furthermore, it would be short-sighted to suggest that only artists and poets

in Kierkegaard's terms, to return to an aesthetic sphere of life, where the imagination (for imagination's sake) is exalted over the practicality, earnestness, and concreteness of actuality. The key to the essentially Christian is the earnest appropriation of the faith: it is obedience to Christ. This is an important reminder—a caveat of sorts—for advocates of the resurgence of the imagination in emergent Christianity. Nonetheless, where an appreciation for the intentional employment of the imagination is entirely lacking, let it be recovered as an essential feature of the essentially Christian and put to use in the service of a more vital, more authentic, and more contextual faith.

Conclusion

Kierkegaard thought highly of the role of the imagination in the cultivation of and practice of the essentially Christian. The modernist approach, as it is reflected in conservative evangelical theology, in its leanings toward literalistic biblical interpretation, didactic preaching, propositional theology, and legalistic moral codes, could be revitalized by a consideration of Kierkegaard's emphasis on the imagination. Furthermore, the modernist impulse, as it shows up in liberal expressions of Christianity, in its emphasis on the primacy of rationality, skepticism of the religious, moralizing, and historical-critical (and demythologizing) approaches to the biblical text, could similarly be challenged by Kierkegaard's articulation of the imagination as channeled through passionate, individual subjectivity and as focused on the paradox of the God-man. Similarly, Kierkegaard's emphasis on the imagination as applied to Scripture could offer a renewed devotional, theological, and transformational use of and interest in the Bible within liberal contexts. Emergent Christianity stands in a unique position to attempt a reinvigoration or a reintegration of the imagination in the practice of the faith—both individually and communally. What Kierkegaard brings—prophetically speaking—to emergent Christianity is the reminder that individual subjectivity, the "solitary individual alone before God," is a crucial element of the essentially Christian. Like anything else, the imagination can become yet another idolatry or ideology. When responsibly, faithfully, and passionately used, however, the imagination can serve as an important catalyst in the revitalization of Christianity.

---

utilize the imagination. For example, any human vocation (i.e., business leaders, architects, educators, etc.) requires at some level the use of the imagination, and therefore suggests that the cultivation of the imagination is a significant endeavor, regardless of the connection to the religious life.

Chapter Four

AGAINST MORALISM

What does it mean to be *human?* What does it mean to be a redeemed and *whole* person and to be saved in and through Christ? In modernity, the fulfillment of a human being's potential was, in some corners at least, determined by the achievement of a disciplined, moral life. The apex of human achievement was individual moral refinement or accomplishment; it places the individual as the central actor in the universe. In *A Secular Age,* philosopher Charles Taylor described moralism as one of the elements of modernity that led to a pervasive unbelief—a swallowing of the transcendent by the immanent. His analysis is worth repeating in full:

> Perhaps the most important for our purposes was the protest against a narrowing of the ends of life to a code of conduct: This ethic of discipline, in both believing and unbelieving variants, was a moralism. It put discipline, self-control, the achieving of a high moral standard as the supreme goal. This tended to be true even of the Evangelical modes, which had after all started in the previous century as a reaction against narrow moralism, for instance in the emotionally liberating preaching of Wesley. Like all moralisms, it could come to seem too thin, too dry, concerned so exclusively with behavior, discipline, control, that it left no space for some great élan or purpose which would transform our lives and take us out of the narrow focus on control. The obsession with getting myself to act right seems to leave no place for some overwhelmingly

important goal or fulfillment, which is the one which gives point to my existence.[1]

Moralism can be seen today in both modernist versions of Christianity, the liberal and the conservative. In the liberal version, tremendous energy and attention are given to ethical or moral practices (such as social justice concerns), whereas the conservative version is preoccupied with the Christian's individual holiness and with preserving—insofar as is possible—"purity" and decency in the public sphere. None of these things are bad, of course, in themselves. They become problematic to the extent that a one-sided emphasis on ethical practices, or a conception of life as determined by ethical concerns, neglects to develop a theology of both the gravity and the relational dimension of sin—as well as a theology of grace that supersedes it. As Taylor noted, moralism can—and did—lead to a diminished sense of sense of need for God and eventually to complete unbelief. Kierkegaard recognized this problem; much of his theology was a response to the "inadequacies of moralism."[2] Kierkegaard's theology of atonement can serve as a useful counter to modernist misconceptions of humanity and of salvation, which are too driven by the impulses of moralism. Moreover, emergent Christians are already rethinking sin—and the theology of the atonement—along more relational and integrated lines while taking into account the priority of grace in salvation; this makes Kierkegaard's theology of atonement—as well as his Christology more broadly—a welcome dialogue partner for emergent theology.

For Kierkegaard, moralism replaces the radicalism of divine forgiveness and love with the delusion of self-justification; it is precluded from the essentially Christian. Sin, rightly understood, cannot be defined solely—or even primarily—with reference to "lawbreaking." Furthermore, a life driven by the impulses of moralism cannot be sustained consistently and authentically over the long term. Nonetheless, Kierkegaard's ethical vision, while precluding moralism, does not abdicate the responsibility of ethical action or the cultivation of virtue. It can inspire a prophetically alternative consciousness that is concerned with issues of both personal holiness and social justice. Kierkegaard's ability to balance the necessity of an active, ethical life (what he calls the "restlessness of faith"), grounded on the realization that everything is made possible through divine grace and forgiveness, is a helpful antidote to much of what plagues modernist

1. Taylor, *Secular Age*, 399.
2. Ibid., 400.

versions of Christianity. Similarly, emergent Christians emphasize the primacy of grace in the Christian life, while—like Kierkegaard—insisting that the authentic experience of grace gives rise to practical obedience.

KIERKEGAARD'S ANTHROPOLOGY: ANXIETY, DESPAIR, AND THE SELF BEFORE GOD

"Sin in man [sic] is like the Greek fire which is not extinguished with water—but in this case only with tears."[3]

Kierkegaard analyzes the "broken heart of modernity" by drilling down to the individual level: to the brokenness of the individual person (the "self" and its relational disruptions).[4] As we have seen, Kierkegaard believed human selfhood is a dynamic process of existential becoming. As the existentialists, influenced by Kierkegaard, consistently affirmed, *existence precedes essence*. The essence of human identity is not a preestablished universal, such as we find in Plato's forms, but is flux—dynamically changing with time and circumstance. Stephen Evans, discussing Kierkegaard's concept of existence, notes that for Kierkegaard, "Human beings do not merely exist in the sense of being actualized in space and time as do rocks and plants, nor merely in the still broader sense of merely having some kind of 'being.' Human existence is a *becoming*; moreover, a special type of becoming."[5]

The dynamic nature of selfhood is illustrated by Kierkegaard's spheres of existence, which progresses conceptually from the aesthetic, to the ethical, to religiousness A (pagan, immanent religiosity), and then to religiousness B, which is the specifically Christian form of religiousness.[6] While guilt is experienced in religiousness A, the consciousness of sin marks the transition between religiousness A and B. But one cannot know what *sin* is apart from divine revelation—knowledge brought in from outside the self.

---

3. *JP* 4, 4008

4. The phrase "broken heart of modernity" comes from Ferguson, *Modernity and Subjectivity*, 149.

5. Evans, *Kierkegaard's "Fragments" and "Postscript,"* cited in Schrag, "Kierkegaard-Effect," 5.

6. The transition from religiousness A to religiousness B involves the recognition of guilt-consciousness as *sin*, which is the admission that "before God one is always in the wrong."

One becomes aware of one's sin—that he or she is a sinner—not by Socratic reflection (the "pagan" understanding of sin as ignorance and of salvation as imparted knowledge), but by the conscious awareness of "how far from perfect you are and what sin is . . ."[7] Kierkegaard, through his pseudonym Anti-Climacus in *Sickness Unto Death*, offers this definition of sin: "Sin is—after being taught by a revelation from God what sin is—before God in despair not to will to be oneself or in despair to will to be oneself."[8] In the Christian sense, sin is defined by the theological notion that all human beings exist "before God."[9] He means by this that because God is infinite and people are finite, we do not "occasionally sin before God"; rather, given the distinction between the finite and the infinite, the consciousness of existing before God involves the recognition that persons are "always guilty."[10] But the awareness is essential: persons are not sinners until they are aware of their existence "before God" and of the "misrelation" between themselves and God; in this awareness, persons make a qualitative leap from anxiety to despair—or guilt-consciousness.

In Christ, God's grace is offered and forgiveness is made available to all; the misrelation is potentially restored through the acceptance of divine forgiveness. But sin is intensified as persons reject the offer of grace. In the words of Anti-Climacus in *Practice in Christianity*, sin is taking "offense" at the paradox (the God-man) and rejecting divine forgiveness. The opposite of sin, we learn in *Sickness Unto Death*, is faith: accepting the forgiveness offered through the God-man is an exercise of faith.[11]

Sin cannot be defined solely by the modernist vocabulary of morality; it is the misrelation of the self to itself, the self to God, and the self to others, which results in a fundamental alienation of the individual and of society as a whole at every level.[12] It emerges from the deep psychology of the self's anxiety, which leads to the deeper existential experience of *despair*. Despair, for Kierkegaard, is the psychological term for the existential realization of guilt (or "guilt-consciousness"). Despair occurs when guilt (a theological reality) is no longer psychologically sup-

---

7. *SUD*, 96.
8. *SUD*, 96.
9. *SUD*, 79–80.
10. *SUD*, 80.
11. *SUD*, 82.
12. *SUD*, 15–16. Kierkegaard works out his analysis of despair as the psychological experience of sin through the perspective of the pseudonym, Anti-Climacus.

pressed. Guilt, however, can be transposed to thankfulness upon encounter with the God-man and the subsequent acceptance of divine forgiveness. In the sphere of religiousness B, this guilt-consciousness (sin) is assuaged by the recognition of and acceptance of divine forgiveness in Jesus Christ, resulting in profound gratitude, or thankfulness. This is why, for Kierkegaard, a person should never wallow in guilt. This sensibility is captured well in a journal entry: "That a person wants to sit and brood and stare at his sin and is unwilling to have faith that it is forgiven: [this is] also guilt in that it is a minimizing of what Christ has done."[13]

This summary of Kierkegaard's complex understanding of the existential development of the self serves to highlight a key point for this chapter: There is a qualitative difference between, on the one side, the ethical and religiousness A and, on the other, religiousness B.[14] Religiousness A is defined by the sphere of immanent religion: one's relation to God is through inwardness and involves the uncovering of innate knowledge (in the mode of Socratic "recollection"—or being made aware, for the first time, of what one innately knows). But in the sphere of religiousness B, something new is brought into the picture: "a God-relationship which is initiated by God breaking into the region of immanence from the outside."[15] A new, transcendent reality is introduced to the immanent sphere by way of divine disclosure and existential encounter. The way to experience this new reality is through the existential embrace of the offer of divine forgiveness and through the relationship of contemporaneity with Christ. The qualitative difference, the infinite gap, between the human and the divine is overcome by God's initiation via contemporaneity with Jesus Christ, who is the perfect synthesis of temporality and eternity. The antidote to despair, and sin as its theological reality "before God," is not morality or ethics, but *faith*. To have faith means that the self relates properly to itself, to others, and to God: it "rests transparently in the power that establishes it."[16]

---

13. *JP* 4, 4036

14. As one author notes, religiousness A "still proceeds hand in glove with the project of the ethically existing subject in process of 'becoming subjective' and appropriating 'truth as subjectivity' through the turn toward inwardness." Schrag, "Kierkegaard-Effect," 8.

15. Ibid. As Johannes Climacus puts it, "In Religiousness B, the upbuilding is something outside the individual; the individual does not find the upbuilding by finding the relationship with God within himself, but relates himself to something outside himself to find the upbuilding" (*CUP*, 561).

16. *SUD*, 14.

KIERKEGAARD ON THE ATONEMENT (SIN AND SALVATION)

"Would that there were a forgiveness, a forgiveness that does not increase my sense of guilt but truly takes the guilt from me, also the consciousness of it."[17]

Kierkegaard did not present a systematic theology of the nature and mechanism of salvation, what theologians call "atonement theory." When he did explicitly refer to the atonement, he generally affirmed aspects of the traditional penal substitution/satisfaction model.[18] Jesus' death on the cross procured forgiveness and removed the guilt that accrued to sinners. Nonetheless, as several scholars have pointed out, Kierkegaard's theology of atonement was more nuanced than a simple restatement of this theory would imply.[19] An understanding of Kierkegaard's theology of the atonement must account for the logical primacy of God's forgiveness rather than God's wrath, holiness, or need for justice.[20] God does not *need* our repentance in order to forgive us—Jesus Christ (the incarnation and Jesus' voluntary death on the cross) is the evidence of that. Traditional penal satisfaction/substitution interpretations of the atonement (common in Reformation Protestant theology) tend to speak of salvation as an economic transaction, fundamentally based in God's need for justice and, consequently, his need for a payment (a punishment) to be exacted in the

---

17. WA, 184.

18. "Christ's death is the atonement for our sins principally by its having made satisfaction for sin. But then one could ask: How could Christ forgive sins while he was alive? This must be explained as an anticipation. There are some differences, however, if Christ forgives sins during his lifetime and if his death is the atonement. In the latter case God the Father is regarded as the one who forgives and Christ as the one who makes satisfaction and thus influences God's willingness to forgive" (JP 2, 1223).

19. See, for example, Walsh, *Kierkegaard: Thinking Christianly*, 131ff.; Law, *Kierkegaard as Negative Theologian*, ch. 7; Sponheim, *Kierkegaard on Christ and Christian Coherence*, ch. 5; and Rae, *Kierkegaard and Theology*, 101–3.

20. Rae notes that Kierkegaard's view "contrasts with the traditional Western *ordo salutis* (order of salvation) in which it is supposed that the process of salvation commences when, in virtue of their own powers of discernment, individuals recognize and repent of their sin. Only then does God offer forgiveness and reconciliation. Grace and forgiveness are presumed to be conditional upon the sinner's contrition. The New Testament, however, has it the other way around. It is in the light of Christ and following the word of forgiveness that the sinner is able to learn what sin is and repent." Rae, *Kierkegaard and Theology*, 100.

stead of the guilty one so that he can forgive. Medieval (Anselmian) satisfaction theory emphasizes the shame that has disrupted the right order of things between God, the "feudal lord," and his subjects. That shame can only be removed through the interposition of a divine-human mediator. For Kierkegaard, however, God has already forgiven us in Christ and has already repaired the relationship. What is lacking is the conscious embrace, or existential appropriation, of that forgiveness by us. A process of existential transformation must occur for a person to come to an awareness of her guilt. But guilt-consciousness is a necessity for the sinner to be reconciled to God, not for God to be reconciled to the sinner. While Kierkegaard's understanding of the atonement accepts the basic thrust of the substitution/satisfaction theories (in that salvation means forgiveness from sin in Jesus Christ), his complex, relational understanding of sin and his focus on salvation as authentic embrace of divine forgiveness results in an atonement theory that emphasizes God's love rather than God's wrath. Furthermore, it prevents a schizophrenic understanding of God, in which God's justice and love are at odds; this view often plagues the substitution/satisfaction theory. Furthermore, Kierkegaard's view of the primacy of forgiveness is a helpful counter to the moralism propagated by an economic theory of the atonement.[21]

Kierkegaard takes sin seriously—but in doing so understands it relationally. Jason Mahn shows that, for Kierkegaard, sin is less something we *do* (as it is in moralism) and more a descriptor of who we *are*—or at least, who we inevitably become. Sin is a "position" rather than an action. Ultimately, sin is, for Kierkegaard, a mystery of human anthropology; but more tangibly, it is the unwillingness to accept the limits of the human condition imposed by our "fortunate fallibility."[22] Kierkegaard terms that unwillingness, in *Sickness unto Death*, "despair." Despair takes two distinct forms: the "masculine form," or the grasping beyond one's creaturely limitations, and the "feminine form," or the unwillingness to live into one's potential as a human being. Both forms reveal a choice (or a succession of choices) borne out of a position in which one refuses to be who one is meant to

21. Like Luther, Kierkegaard, reflecting on Luther's sermons, noted that the doctrine of forgiveness pushes well beyond moralism—it must be understood in the context of the existential God-relationship. As he stated, ". . . sins' forgiveness belongs to the pure God-relationship, far beyond sin—and virtue. The forgiveness of sin is a totality-qualification based on my being in relationship to God" (*JP* 2, 1218). See also *JP* 2, 1206, 1205, 1209, 1216, and 1223.

22. See Mahn, *Fortunate Fallibility*.

be, a human being "before God." Sin is actualized as sin when a person is unwilling to embrace Christ's forgiveness. As Kierkegaard's Anti-Climacus, in *Practice in Christianity*, urges again and again, the sinner is confronted with a choice to embrace the paradox (that God has become incarnate in this single human being) and to follow Jesus in suffering, or to refuse to accept the paradox ("to take offense"). The despairing sinner consciously refuses what is offered in Jesus: a journey of a radical reorientation toward God, oneself, and others.

In Kierkegaard's view of sin, we are drawn into a complex, deeply integrated, relationally defined space "beyond both moralism and iconoclasm, the ethical and the aesthetic," where we are called to be "both spirited and good."[23] To be spirited means to exert one's freedom and to live decisively in the face of complex, finite, and even "sinful" realities where, as Mahn suggests, one must risk "ethical and spiritual failure . . ."[24] In the midst of this ambiguous, challenging journey of risky decisiveness where "moral failure" is inevitable, a person finds both hope and forgiveness in the liturgy—in the Eucharist in particular. A Christian venturing to live authentically, by following the God-man, exists in the liturgical interim of Holy Saturday, that place of existential crisis and "unknowing" between death and resurrection. Human fallibility is necessary for experiencing faith—but it also invites the crisis of disbelief and the rejection of God. Salvation is not a mere economic transition, in which our debts are cleared. Rather, it is a holistic, relational transformation in which we become "forgiven sinners" in Christ.[25]

While we might wish Kierkegaard had straightened out some of the ambiguity in his own atonement theology (and while other theologians take us much further in this than Kierkegaard), the tension reflected in his approach offers deeper rationale for courageous, ethical action than what we find in many articulations of the substitution/satisfaction atonement theories. In Kierkegaard's theology, the primacy of God's love and the actuality of divine forgiveness grant no license for ethical laxity. The rigorous demands of discipleship and of the essentially Christian cannot be sidestepped. Nor, however, is there vindication of self-justification or validation of moralism as a defining way of life. Kierkegaard's christocentric view of the atonement, coupled with a rigorous theology of sin, prevents a collapse into either the heavy-handed, judgmental God of Reformed

23. Ibid., 20.
24. Ibid.
25. Ibid., 156.

orthodoxy on one side, or the naïve self-righteousness of Pelagian moralism on the other. Kierkegaard challenges us to be "spirited and good," to venture boldly in response to the freedom procured by God's forgiveness.

Is There a "Universal" Ethical Binding on Us All?

For Kierkegaard, in the sphere of religiousness B, ethical concerns are not dropped; rather, they are elevated. In this higher key, ethics must be interpreted in relation both to the absolute of eternity and to the relativity and contingency of temporality. In this sense, ethical principles and moral rules (even the law) ought not to be universalized and made the highest ideal of human achievement. Kierkegaard perceived the notion of the universal ethical to be endemic to Hegelian, immanent forms of Christianity. Hegelianism (as did Kantianism) turned God, the Lord of history, into a kind of ethical principle embedded in the fabric of the finite world. God's transcendence was reduced to the human religiosity of moral activity. In *Fear and Trembling*, Kierkegaard (via Johannes de Silentio) famously critiqued this Hegelian reduction of God and immanentizing of the God-relationship. The figure of Abraham, the "knight of faith," was used to make the point that one's individual relationship to God may require a "teleological suspension of the [universal] ethical" so that the demands of paradoxical, passionate faith can be met. God's command for Abraham to sacrifice Isaac, though ultimately withdrawn, illustrates the notion that a universal ethical principle cannot usurp the primacy of the God-relationship and cannot be the primary criterion of a person's religious life. In short, the ethical life cannot constitute—in full or in any final way—the essentially Christian.

In the quest for an authentic faith, a system of morality (moralism) can itself become an idol that requires deconstruction. Mark Dooley points out that Levinas' critique of Kierkegaard's ethics, on the basis of his discussion of Abraham in *Fear and Trembling*, is misguided. Levinas fails to recognize that Kierkegaard's suspension of the ethical is a not an abrogation of ethics, but its *teleological* suspension (meaning it was both temporary and purposeful). Kierkegaard was not positing the irrelevance of ethical activity and moral responsibility; rather, he was "reconfiguring" it in light of the contingency of history and the priority of subjectivity over universality. Contra Hegel's impulse to interpret the development of ethics within history as the unfolding of the immanent Spirit, Kierkegaard resisted universalizing "the ethical" over the "needs of singularity," or the "interests of existing individuals."[26] Dooley rightly notes that Kierkegaard's philosophy of ethics has more relevance for our postmodern situation than he is typically given credit for. He overstates, however, the conflict between the Lutheran theology Kierkegaard inherited (which prioritizes grace over law and supposedly revels in the "freedom" from ethical responsibility) and his more earnest—even if occasional and contextual—ethic. It is true that Kierkegaard's understanding of faith as giving rise to ethical responsibility was a *correction* of the inadequacies—or perversions—of Lutheran theology. But Kierkegaard believed he was returning ethical reflection to the spirit of Luther's original understanding of the gospel. Christendom—with its lax, apathetic ethical vision—had misunderstood, or misapplied, Luther. In what follows, we take a closer look at how Kierkegaard, particularly in his explicit "signed" writings and in his journal reflections, understood—following Luther himself—the gospel as a dialectical relationship between ethical striving and the reality of grace, which, far from negating ethical action, raises it to a higher key. This higher key excludes moralism as a defining feature of the essentially Christian.

The New Testament: Difficult to Understand or Difficult to Follow?

Particularly in his later years (his "second authorship") and into his *Attack Upon Christendom*, Kierkegaard sought to offer a corrective to what he perceived to be two key misunderstandings regarding what constitutes New Testament Christianity: (1) the primacy of moral or ethical rigor (or *moralism*) in the Christian life, in which one assumes that one's actions have "merit," and (2) moral or ethical laxity, which assumes that because one has salvation or is already a Christian, there is nothing more to be done—nothing more is required. Kierkegaard tried to bring the theology of Paul and James back together again as dialectical (and equally essential) aspects of the essentially Christian.

In Kierkegaard's view, Christendom had misinterpreted the authentic nature of the truly Christian way of discipleship. The "higher" (the strenuous, rigorous way of Christianity) was viewed, by the state-church theologians and leaders, as the "fantastical" and "ludicrous exaggeration," while the "lower" (the reasoned, careful, "sagacious" approach to Christianity)

26. See the introduction to Dooley, *Politics of Exodus*, especially xviii–xix.

was misconstrued as the way of wisdom. For Kierkegaard, the message of the New Testament, with its concepts of sin and guilt, redemption and salvation, had to be understood in accordance with the life-view presupposed and presented in the New Testament. Kierkegaard wanted, in his own words, to bring people "a little more truth (in the direction of being persons of ethical and ethical-religious character, of renouncing worldly sagacity, of being willing to suffer for the truth, etc.), which indeed is always something and in any case is the first condition for beginning to exist more capably . . ." He wanted to "prevent people in 'Christendom' from existentially taking in vain Luther and the significance of Luther's life . . ."[27]

Kierkegaard sought to preserve the biblical dialectic between grace and ethical responsibility. Nonetheless, this was a fragile task, because ethical striving can easily lead to self-justification and to the assumption that one has achieved "merit" before God. In an extended reflection on the "tax collector" forgiven by Jesus, Kierkegaard noted that he "completely agree[s] with Luther" that even if a person committed "horrible crimes," if he simply said, "God, be merciful to me, a sinner" he "may count himself indescribably happy compared with the person who, making every sacrifice for the truth in greatest possible self-denial for an entire lifetime, for one single moment made the mistake of thinking he had merit before God."[28] For Kierkegaard, it is worse to assume that one has achieved merit before God than it is to be a notorious sinner. Kierkegaard was after basic honesty in people: an "admission" that they did not match up to the requirements of the New Testament, modeled in the "prototype," Jesus Christ. The New Testament commands obedience to Christ and the imitation of Christ. But the intention of the gospel is not to "crush" the striver. Rather, "its intention is that by means of the requirement and my humiliation I shall be lifted, believing and worshiping—and then I am light as a bird."[29] Even the thought of God's grace is uplifting.[30]

27. *POV,* 16–17.
28. *JFY,* 198.
29. *JFY,*153.
30. Consider the following entry regarding how the New Testament ideal works to awaken realization of sin and the existential need for grace: "In regard to all existential [*existentiel*] knowing, the main thing is to bring about the situation. This is what people have completely forgotten, and for this reason they cannot get an impression of Christianity. I am thinking of a man who so far does not have any impression of Christianity and is not deeply gripped by the sense of his sin but lives on in the comfortable notion that he is still going to be saved. Let him then take and read the New Testament. No

The New Testament Kierkegaard presents is a rigorous one indeed. But this light of grace sparkles, illuminates, and penetrates the prescription. That is an uplifting thought. Kierkegaard knew that only through faith are we justified; but justifying faith is a striving faith, a struggling faith, a "restless" faith. Kierkegaard had found a concrete, existential way to fit grace and works together such that the New Testament dialectic remained in a splendid tension while demanding a rigorous, realistic, and passionately inward relationship to it. Kierkegaard's understanding of the relationship between grace and works suggests that the authentic Christian life should attend to ethical concerns and to matters of social justice, without idolizing those ethical-social practices. We are all sinners—we all remain sinners; the question is whether we are forgiven (and thus "restless") sinners or despairing sinners who are resigned to inaction. In short, the function of the New Testament, in Kierkegaard's understanding, includes ethical/character formation and a vision for a social application of the ethical-religious life.

Faith Is a "Restless" Thing: The Ethical Outworking of Inward Salvation

The preceding discussion raises a number of questions. Kierkegaard sought a dialectical, but integrated, theology of faith expressed in "works"; faith naturally gives rise to active, outward, ethical-religious action. Genuine faith is *restless*—and therefore is active. But in what sense does Kierkegaard lead us today in living out a prophetic Christian witness in the public or social sphere? To put it another way: How does Kierkegaard encourage Christians to act in favor of justice and against injustice or oppression in the world? To get at this question more fully, we will have to await the next chapter, where we elaborate on Kierkegaard's statement that the discourses in *Works of Love* are his vision of authentic subjectivity applied externally and socially. Kierkegaard was cognizant that his emphasis on the individual person "before God" and the primacy of subjectivity in his thought could

---

one can deny that the ethical teaching presented here is such that it moves the imagination of every man. Well, now, let him begin there. He carries out his intention to realize Christianity.... But look, because he carries it out, he will in a Christian way collide with the world; he will be abused as an egotist just when he acts more disinterestedly, etc. Now the pinch comes, now he cannot hold out alone—now he must have religious help.... See, now the matter is in full swing; now he needs grace; now he needs Christ" (*JP* 1, 513).

Against Moralism

be interpreted in a very limited way and could end up being utilized as justification for yet another iteration of Christendom, where everything becomes inward (with a palpable lack of rigor and passion), and not externally expressed.

Kierkegaard's understanding of sin as misrelation implies that there are visible, positive consequences to the restoration of relationships. A new orientation toward God, self, and others is manifested in ethical concern and in a valuing of the "other"—not as distant or inferior, but as one's *neighbor*. In community, one learns to appreciate the diversity of ways in which the subjectivity of others is lived out. It is not my place to determine the consequences and implications of another person's God-relationship. It is not my place to determine how another person should interpret Scripture, under the guidance of the Holy Spirit. And yet, we ought not to relinquish the duty we have in Christian community to edify others and to be edified by them. In community we learn to act justly and lovingly toward each other. Nonetheless, for Kierkegaard, there can be no ethical universal that usurps the primacy of the God-relationship—the single individual "before God" who in fear and trembling must determine what is right and good in any given situation.[31] History flows, times change, situations alter; when existence precedes essence, not much is set in stone. To elucidate this point further, we will bring Kierkegaard's critique of moralism into conversation with postmodern theology and emergent Christianity.

KIERKEGAARD, CAPUTO, AND THE "GOOD GHOST" OF JUSTICE

John Caputo shows how, in the philosophy of Jacques Derrida, the dialectical relationship between justice and law challenges moralism as a way of life. For Derrida, known as the "father of deconstruction," the only reality

---

31. The discussion puts us face to face with an important discussion regarding the place (or lack thereof) for ethics in Kierkegaard's religious philosophy. Alasdair MacIntyre prompted a number of passionate responses when he suggested that Kierkegaard was an irrational fideist who separated entirely rational reflection from the ethical life. Kierkegaard scholars have rightly shown this interpretation of Kierkegaard to be a misunderstanding of the relation between reason and faith in Kierkegaard's thought as well as the role for ethics in his view of the religious life. Kierkegaard's critique of the "ethical universal" must be understood in the context of his quibble with a particular form of Enlightenment rationalism in Hegelian thought. See Davenport, Rudd, MacIntyre, and Quinn, *Kierkegaard After MacIntyre*.

that is not deconstructible is justice.³² We pray for, work toward, and long for justice—justice feels transcendent, basic, and necessary. Laws, on the other hand, simply exist as historical, concrete—but "repealable."³³ They can and should be amended in accordance with the "good ghost of justice," which "haunts the laws," calling them toward justice."³⁴ The dialectic between the concreteness (but repealability) of laws and the pervasiveness of justice is a necessary tension. The construction of a universal, unbending, unchanging set of rules (making law universal and absolute) is unwise and destructive. People desire—or should desire—a "justice with the force of law and laws that answer to the call of justice."³⁵

Derrida's notion, as Caputo describes it, fits well with Kierkegaard's "teleological suspension of the ethical," in which the universal ethical is subordinated to the desire of justice—which is ultimately determined and articulated in the context of the God-relationship. It is difficult for us to imagine murdering one's child, even on the "command" of God, as an expression of justice. Nonetheless, Kierkegaard's insistence on the primacy of the God-relationship for the ethical life must be understood as his way of highlighting the contingency of law, of morality, in relation to the deeper reality of God's relation to humanity in the flux and flow of history.³⁶ To borrow from Caputo: the "good ghost" of (God's) justice permeates and relativizes the law—and destabilizes moralism as an ultimate way of life.

Caputo also connects deconstruction with the theme of forgiveness—a key theme for Derrida in his later years. For Derrida, forgiveness cannot be understood or practiced within an economic system of debt and payment. Forgiveness is truly a gift, which means that "the only condition under which true forgiveness is possible is when forgiveness is impossible."³⁷ In other words, forgiveness is a paradoxical matter of grace, not an economic transaction. The grace and gift-orientation of forgiveness is contrary, Caputo notes, to the ways in which Christianity and Judaism have often behaved: "like bankers when it comes to forgiveness."³⁸ Provided the *if-then*

32. Caputo, *What Would Jesus Deconstruct?*, 63.
33. Ibid.
34. Ibid., 64–65.
35. Ibid., 65.
36. Furthermore, it is important to keep in mind that, in the end, God told Abraham to withhold the knife.
37. Caputo, *What Would Jesus Deconstruct?*, 73
38. Ibid.

conditions are met, the debt can be forgiven. Like Caputo, for Kierkegaard, divine forgiveness does not work this way. Instead, as Kierkegaard himself noted, forgiveness leads to repentance: Love "loves forth love."[39] Love, not law, elicits active repentance. Genuine forgiveness, as Caputo notes—and as Kierkegaard affirms—is a *gift*, not a "deal."[40]

The picture of divine forgiveness in the New Testament (*gift* rather than economic exchange) shows the inadequacy of a reductively penal substitution or satisfaction view of the atonement. As we have seen, Kierkegaard affirmed aspects of the traditional view: Christ's death was a sacrifice for our sin, and in that sense Christ was a "substitute" for us. But his Christology (Jesus as the paradoxical God-man who invites followers), his emphasis on the radical nature of divine love, and his prioritizing of forgiveness suggests that a Kierkegaardian theology of sin and atonement shares commonalities with the direction of postmodern theology and of emergent Christianity. Keeping Kierkegaard's prophetic dimension in mind, however, we should note that the seriousness of sin in light of the necessity of divine forgiveness ought not to be forgotten. In the deconstruction of moralism as a defining way of being Christian, emergent leaders ought not to neglect the severity of sin and the central role Christ plays in redemption and salvation.

AN EMERGENT THEOLOGY OF THE ATONEMENT

In their discussion of the atonement, emergent leaders favor moving away from economic metaphors and themes and toward relational ones. In his essay "The Emerging Church and Embodied Theology," Doug Pagitt argues that God's intention in salvation is "to bring together full integration of God's agenda with our world." Sin is "dis-integration," but God desires "integration."[41] He suggests that a model of forgiveness based on the economic metaphor is "built around a Greek judicial model of separation rather than around a relational call to return to a life in full agreement and rhythm with God." God does not "move away" from us in our sin; rather, "he moves closer."[42] In *A Christianity Worth Believing*, Pagitt notes that the economic model "hamstrings God," because it makes God "beholden to the

---

39. *WL*, 217.
40. Caputo, *What Would Jesus Deconstruct?*, 74.
41. Pagitt, "Emerging Church and Embodied Theology," 132.
42. Ibid., 134.

law," when in fact the converse is true.[43] This may be another way of putting Caputo's (and Derrida's) point: justice, not law, is undeconstructible.

The gospel, according to Pagitt, is about relationships, not legality. The judicial (economic) model of the atonement "puts the law at the center of the story," making "love, grace, mercy, compassion, goodness, and even God" only "minor players." In an economic framework, "the gospel itself becomes less about God and more about the sin problem."[44] The disruption of relationship caused by sin cannot be resolved by recourse to the law, or to the framework of moralism. Moralism may only cause further disruption of relationship, or at minimum may simply lead to a relational standstill or prevention of a breakthrough toward abundant life.[45] For Pagitt, sin does not cause problems for God so much as it does for people who, because of their sin, refuse to relate rightly to God.[46] But God cares about providing redemption from sin through Jesus and offers the possibility of new life through divine forgiveness. In Jesus, God offers the integration of what has been dis-integrated.

Similarly, Karen Ward, in her essay "The Emerging Church and Communal Theology," asks whether there is such a thing as an "emerging theology" of the atonement.[47] She suggests that, while there is not, emerging thinkers have a unique way of "interfacing with the doctrine of the atonement." The atonement may best be understood not with reference to propositional theology (systematic theology), but through engagement in "art, ritual, community, etc."[48] Correct theology cannot save us; the modernist preoccupation with the mechanism and the "order" of salvation is misguided. Instead, Scripture invites us to participate in its images and narratives of marveling at the mystery and splendor of the incarnation of Jesus and the power of the Spirit. In composing her essay, Ward invited

---

43. Pagitt, *Christianity Worth Believing*, 151.

44. Ibid., 155.

45. Pagitt raises an example of someone whose sister is "stuck in an awful abusive marriage"; he cannot tell her to get out and get help because "the Bible says divorce is wrong." Another example is a woman who had an abortion and, later in life, cannot come to grips with God's forgiveness—she thinks "God is still angry with me for disobeying him." Ibid., 153–54.

46. As he puts it, "sin isn't a legal problem with God; it's a relationship problem with us." Ibid., 159.

47. Fittingly, Ward points out that the essay was written in collaboration with members of her church community, because "that is how we operate . . ." (161).

48. Ward, "Emerging Church and Communal Theology," 164.

members of her community to reflect on the meaning of the atonement. These reflections highlighted the "event-nature" of the atonement and emphasized its nature as mystery:

> You are invited into a mystery.... You are invited to lay down your theories and enter in.... Swallow the red pill, taste and see the "Pascal reality"—the salvific action of Christ—past, present, and future, that is shared with us in the gospel story, and into which we are invited to know and experience.[49]

We are invited to "enter atonement *as a happening in God, to God, and through God,* and for our sake, breaking open and making possible a new way to live life."[50] This means that atonement is a relational and community-enabled experience of embracing the newness that comes in Christ. The atonement is an "event" that is *lived,* or experienced, more than it is believed and understood: "To be saved or atoned for is to have and experience a love relationship with God that is evidenced by living in a loving manner here upon the earth, as 'God is love.'"[51]

Emergent Christians reflect the attempt to rethink the gospel apart from the inordinate influence of the traditional penal substitution/satisfaction atonement theory. Scot McKnight, who has been articulating a more robust, holistic, and "biblical" understanding of the atonement, points out that emergent leaders are trying to connect Jesus' preaching of "the gospel of the kingdom" with Paul's preaching of "the gospel of salvation and justification by faith."[52] Traditional evangelical theology has emphasized, by default, Paul's theory of justification. As Brian McLaren suggests, these evangelicals have interpreted Paul through the grid of Luther's Reformation theology—a penal substitution framework organized around judicial, forensic, and economic metaphors.[53] Emergent Christians are dissatisfied with the individualism and escapism fostered by the nearly exclusively penal substitution understanding of the gospel. When the gospel is reduced to the acquisition of one's personal salvation and to securing one's personal, eternal homecoming in heaven, a sense of the cosmic, collective nature of the gospel is lost. Furthermore, it is hard to see how one's relation to the

---

49. Ibid. This particular quotation was contributed to their collaborative blog by Phil Woodward (October 13, 2005).

50. Ibid.

51. Ibid., 165.

52. McKnight, "Atonement and Gospel," 124.

53. McLaren, *New Kind of Christianity,* 137–46.

atonement becomes anything other than individualist, perhaps even narcissistic or self-centered. Brian McLaren suggests that the Bible nowhere speaks of "accep[ting] Jesus Christ as your personal savior."[54] A focus on procuring individual salvation (from hell and into heaven) misses the point:

> To Paul the point of being Christ's follower was not just to help people be absolutely certain they were going to heaven after they died. Paul's goal was to help them become fully formed, mature in Christ, here and now—to experience the glorious realities of being in Christ and experiencing Christ in themselves.[55]

Salvation in the Bible, McLaren reminds us, has a horizontal as well as a vertical dimension. In the Old Testament, it includes "rescue from sickness, trouble, distress, fear, or (this especially) from enemies and their violence."[56] God saves people from real-world oppression, not just from the vertical (divine-human) aspect of sin. Salvation is certainly not the salvation of God from himself (as in some "schizophrenic" forms of penal substitution theory). This rediscovery of the significance of the horizontal dimension of the gospel is based in an affirmation of the creational significance of this life. When a "future life" is prioritized in an escapist theology of salvation, the meaning of the temporal/historical is threatened. The full humanity of our experience gives way to a docetic devaluing of our human nature. The experience of suffering becomes a phantasm—a temporary nuisance on the path to our eternal salvation.

Peter Rollins suggests that emerging churches seek to counter this gospel reduction with a robust theology of the incarnation; the inherent goodness of creation and of humanity—affirmed by a solid doctrine of the incarnation—counters this docetic, gnostic error. Rollins cites Bonhoeffer's suggestion that the true affirmation of Christianity and the authenticity of faith depends on the validation of the full human experience, including the experience of human suffering: "For 'that is faith, that is *metanoia* and that is what makes a [person] and a Christian.'"[57]

In this regard, Rollins might as well have cited Kierkegaard, for whom the incarnation—the absolute paradox—means that God so values the frailties of the human experience that he voluntarily enters into history and

---

54. McLaren and Campolo, *Adventures in Missing the Point*, 19

55. Ibid., 20.

56. Ibid.

57. Bonhoeffer, *Letters and Papers from Prison*, 486; cited in Rollins, "Worldly Theology of Emerging Christianity," 36.

becomes the suffering or "abased" one. New Testament Christianity is an invitation to follow Jesus on the pathway of suffering—not to hide from suffering but to embrace it as an affirmation of finitude's beauty. Christians are invited to follow in the way of their "pattern," Jesus Christ, who defines the gospel by his *kenotic* (self-emptying) love. Furthermore, the gospel of the incarnation means that Christians and the church are called to recognize their sin, embrace the forgiveness offered in Jesus, venture boldly in works of courageous faith, and reject moralism as a way of life. The following statement sums up the significance of rethinking the gospel along these *gospel* (Jesus-centered) lines: "In concrete terms, emerging church leaders look to Jesus as the one who initiated the work of the kingdom in Israel, and their hope is to point to the kingdom through their communal practices in postmodern culture today."[58] Here we also get a taste for what will follow in the next chapter, "Reclaiming Love."

The emergent church rightly attempts to correct an overly vertical and judicial understanding of the gospel by highlighting the holistic, this-worldly, and Jesus-centered nature of the kingdom of God. Nonetheless, in so doing, emergent Christians—particularly its theologians and leaders—should take care not to minimize the reality of sin and its effects, not solely with respect to the vertical divine-human relationship, but also with respect to the relationship between persons and themselves (the psychological/spiritual), between persons and others, and between persons and their environment. The severity, mystery, and tragedy of sin needs consistently to be affirmed, addressed, and proclaimed.

Tony Jones, in his recent book *The Church Is Flat*, makes this point as well. Since it is a self-contained and significant statement, coming from one of the movement's most visible theologians, I reproduce the quote here in full:

> The emerging church also places a high level of trust in fellow human beings and in the technology that connects people in the twenty-first century. Both the polity that is developing in the ECM (emerging church movement), and the embrace of social media as a means for connecting with one another betray a possible naiveté

---

58. Gibbs and Bolger, *Emerging Churches*, 48. Gibbs and Bolger cite Emergent leader Mark Scandrette (ReIMAGINE! church, San Francisco): "Most harbor hostility to the Christian faith. We want to help people consider Jesus as an option through the beauty of how we live our lives. Living in the way of Jesus is not a belief system but a reality. We believe in an 'inhabited apologetic,' and through our lives 'we bear witness to the reality of God'" (58).

> about the nature of human relationships. What is not often heard in these churches is talk about the traditional Western doctrine of original sin, much less the Reformed doctrine of total depravity. Instead, there seems to be a generally optimistic view about humankind. How the movement will deal with the inevitable foibles of its members and leaders remains to be seen. Again, it seems that some cogent theological reflection on this matter would serve the movement well.[59]

Jones seems to be responding to a perceived lack of serious engagement with the doctrine of sin in emerging churches, "on the ground." As I have been suggesting, the thought leaders of emergent Christianity do recognize a role for sin in articulating an atonement theology, though much more could be said. As I have argued throughout this chapter, perhaps Kierkegaard can offer a prophetic voice in pursuing the very task that Jones mentioned, because he attends, in an integrated way, to theological, philosophical, and psychological understandings of the reality of sin. Perhaps in that reflection on the reality of sin and the profundity of divine forgiveness, the inadequacies of modernistic moralism can be clearly perceived. At the same time, the seriousness of sin—and its "disintegrative" consequences—should be consistently affirmed, with divine forgiveness and human repentance offered as proper responses. For Christians, there is no way around sin but through the cross.

Conclusion

One of Kierkegaard's many enduring contributions to modern theology was his critique of moralism as a defining, organizing principle of life. Kierkegaard, who was thoroughly motivated by his understanding of the New Testament, knew that individuals cannot experience genuine salvation by exerting their moral sensibilities—by attempting to follow "universal" moral laws or principles. He also knew that the "broken heart of modernity" could not be healed through a collective, moral, or ethical consciousness. In these senses, Kierkegaard also anticipated the objections of postmodernity to the "totalizing" impulses of moralism. When moralism rules, those in charge get to set the agenda of what counts as morality. Thus, in the same way that Foucault said "power is knowledge," so "power is morality." For Kierkegaard, however, morality submits to the primacy

---

59. Jones, *Church Is Flat*, 123.

of the existential (subjectively oriented) God-relationship. The contours of legitimate action and the motivations of our passionate, ethical lives are determined and driven by the context of our relationships to and with God (and, derivatively, to and with each other). The Spirit guides us into truth—and into ethical action.

This way of framing the motivation of ethical action must be sourced in a integrated understanding of *sin* as the reason for the fragmentation of self and society. The answer to the sin problem is confession—to Jesus Christ—in the context of a community of Christ-followers. Emergent church leaders must recognize that the power and profundity of sin cannot be discounted. Sin's power is dealt with through atonement with Christ. Christ forgives sin (indeed, he has *already* forgiven sin), leading to repentance and transformation. Ultimately, however, atonement—like sin—is a mystery that must be engaged more than it can be understood.

Kierkegaard's theology of sin, salvation, and ethics applied to the emerging church context does not negate moral action and ethical concern. To the contrary, it ensures that ethical action has its basis in divine forgiveness and emerges out of the actuality of love. This love is not a triumphalist or patronizing love, but a love modeled after the "pattern," Jesus Christ. In the next chapter, we explore the nature of that love and the ways in which it issues forth in a postmodern apologetic of *witness*.

Chapter Five

RECLAIMING LOVE

"O Eternal Love, you who are everywhere present and never without witness where you are called upon, be not without witness in what will be said here about love or about works of love."[1]

For Kierkegaard, the essentially Christian is defined by the passion of authentic inwardness and by the subjective appropriation of truth. This approach entails that the vocation of the Christian and the church be an ethic of witness defined by its orientation to the God-man. This humble, other-centered witness is the offspring of the existential acceptance of divine forgiveness and of the earnest attempt to follow Jesus, the prototype or "pattern." This ethic of witness is qualitatively different from moralism, in that it precludes self-justification and does not pin its hopes for transformation on adherence to an abstract, universal moral code, but on the actuality of the imitation of Jesus Christ. In this chapter, I develop that implication further, exploring Kierkegaard's development of this ethic of witness biblically in terms of neighbor-love, in which God is conceived as the "middle term."[2] This ethic of witness has as its governing principle, as

---

1. *WL*, 4.
2. When God is the "middle term," one's actions toward another are filtered through the grid of the God-relationship, which means that in consequence of making love for God the priority, all human beings are equally valued and loved. See *WL*, 57–58, 106–9.

do all Christian practices, the biblical injunction to love God and neighbor. Following the example of Christ on the cross, this witness is a *kenotic* witness that, while not minimizing central religious convictions, approaches the task of witness through the posture of humility, concern for the other, and suffering for truth. Kierkegaard's witness of love precludes ideological violence and upholds, in a sacred trust, the good of the other.

THE PRIMACY OF LOVE AND CHRIST AS THE "PATTERN"

In this section we arrive at what might be called the center of Kierkegaard's prophetic Christian consciousness: his Christology. For Kierkegaard, the absolute paradox signifies God becoming a single, particular, historical human being in Jesus Christ; this singularity—and the epistemological gap between the historical past and the present—implies that authentic relatedness to God requires passionate faith. The passion of faith differs from the modernist approach of relating to God via human rationality (whether skepticism, propositionalism, or bibliolatry), empirical proof, or moralism. In a departure from objective versions of Christianity, Kierkegaard reminds us that relating to Christ in faith as a *person* is more important than believing a doctrine or a set doctrines about him. Kierkegaard insisted, "Christ is infinitely more important than his teaching."[3] Being (or, better, *becoming*) a Christian involves following Christ more than it involves believing theological concepts. The former is the sphere of action, of "praxis," whereas the latter is the sphere of reflection, a form of systematic, or dogmatic, theology that is detached from the actuality of the world.

For Kierkegaard, the gospel teaching of the imitation of Christ is a dividing line that separates the disciple from the pagan; it "is really the point from which the human race shrinks."[4] Christ does not want admirers but disciples; Judas and Nicodemus were admirers: "the *disciple* is the criterion; imitation and Christ as the prototype must be affirmed" as the measure, in order to awaken one's self-awareness to one's finitude and sinfulness.[5] Kierkegaard admitted that were he to be measured by the prototype, he would prove to be the "dunce of the class." The good news, however (the *gospel* is good news to the one who strives), is that while "the prototype

3. *PC*, 124
4. *JFY*, 188.
5. *JFY*, 199

requires imitation," "by his *reconciliation*" he "expels, if possible, all anxiety from a person's soul."[6] Grace, in the form of reconciliation, accompanies the command of imitation and saves us from our inability to consistently follow the prototype. As we attempt to follow the way of Christ's *kenotic*, suffering love—with utmost concern for the neighbor, or the "other"—we must always remain aware of the presence of grace. Yet, as we also discovered, this grace is no license for laxity. The essentially Christian will have outward, tangible effects.

Kierkegaard noted in a late journal entry, "What God wanted through Christianity was a transformation of the world, but a transformation of the actual, the practical world." This real-world transformation stands contrary to what Kierkegaard called "playing at Christianity," where in hidden inwardness, or "on Sundays," one makes a "fool of God."[7] The essentially Christian is marked by its concern for the practical, the actual, and on behalf of the "world." This concern is perfectly reflected in the life of Jesus of Nazareth, and it is the goal of the divine command to love one's neighbor as oneself.

Works of Love That Change the World through Conflict with the World

"Will not true Christianity or Christianity in character produce the same effect in every age, the effect that is foretold in the New Testament: persecution—is this not the view of the N.T.?"[8]

In *Works of Love*, Kierkegaard upholds the performance of works of love in the social sphere as the primary theme of Christianity. He explained that he wrote the discourses that comprise *Works of Love* precisely to show how genuine subjectivity and the essentially Christian plays out relationally, or socially, when one has an adequate theology of love.[9] Christian (or divine)

6. *JFY*, 209.
7. *JP* 1, 541
8. *TM*, 480.
9. In a journal entry from 1847, less than a year before Kierkegaard published *Works of Love*, he wrote, "Despite everything people ought to have learned about my maieutic carefulness, by proceeding slowly and continually letting it seem as if I knew nothing more, not the next thing—now on the occasion of my new upbuilding discourses they will probably bawl out that I do not know what comes next, that I know nothing about

Reclaiming Love

love [*Kjerlighed*], Kierkegaard urged, is not defined by sentimentality or erotic attraction, as is erotic love [*Elskov*]. Furthermore, love is not defined by human preference. Kierkegaard distinguished between "divine love" and "merely human love"; the latter is based on preferentiality—people naturally love others for what they offer in return. We love others for their beauty, for their fame, for their humor, etc., because in loving them we receive pleasure, confidence, security, or social status. Divine love, on the other hand, is not motivated by what one receives in return; it is a natural outflow of God's nature. When people act in accordance with divine love, they are merely responding to divine command: "you shall love!" Love, then, is a duty rather than a sentimental, emotional, or sensual response to an attractive object. Neighbor-love is a manifestation of divine love, when lived out socially and relationally—it is the horizontal aspect of the gospel. True neighbor-love is, in a sense, completely devoid of preferential treatment. Kierkegaard was careful to clarify that the "neighbor" is not the person who lives close to you; the neighbor is anyone (and everyone) you might come across. The neighbor is an anonymous person in need. When acting in accordance with divine love, one loves the anonymous neighbor no less than one loves a family member, lover, or close friend. This egalitarian, nonpreferential treatment is illustrated in Kierkegaard's suggestion that we "wear our garments loosely"; a particular challenge of neighbor-love is transcending socioeconomic distinctions. Whether one is "royalty" or a "beggar" matters not one iota with respect to the essentially Christian.[10] Kierkegaard illustrated this in the figure of the beggar named Lazarus in the Gospel of Luke, who sat outside the gate of the rich man (whom tradition has called Dives).[11] In the afterlife, their situations were reversed: Lazarus lived comfortably in the "bosom of Abraham," whereas the rich man suffered in the desolation and heat, longing for a drop of water. In

---

sociality. . . . Now I have the theme of the next book. It will be called: *Works of Love*" (*Pap.* VIII1 A 4). Kierkegaard was expressing here that his emphasis on subjectivity and the single individual is not *reductively* individualist, but has an external, relational, and *social* application.

10. WL, 88–89.

11. Kierkegaard used this figure in several of his religious discourses, including the *Four Upbuilding Discourses, Upbuilding Discourses in Various Spirits,* and *Works of Love*. For an analysis of his use of Lazarus to convey the distinctiveness of the "world of the spirit"—reality as interpreted through the lens of authentic Christianity—see Roberts, "Lazarus."

the world of the spirit, Kierkegaard proclaimed, all are equal.[12] This means that the leprous beggar ought not to be denied basic human rights and the rich have a responsibility to care for the unfortunate. Furthermore, in the context of the spirit of *Works of Love*, it means that Christians have a duty, individually and collectively, to follow the pattern set by Christ: to love one's enemies and to care for the "least of these."

Kierkegaard believed that the corruption of the current age (Christendom) had forgotten that Jesus Christ is the ideal, the pattern, and that the essentially Christian requires making a decisive break with the world; the kingdom Jesus proclaimed "wants to be a stranger in life because it belongs to another world . . ."[13] Love and the Christian mission, which Kierkegaard called "the change of infinity," has made relationships matters of conscience—of *duty*—with God as the "middle term."[14] The God-relationship is the criterion for how one treats the other: there can be no preferential treatment when it comes to Christian love. Through the deepening of inwardness and subjectivity, Christianity "wants to transform all love into a matter of conscience."[15] This transformation makes Christianity a "stranger" in the world—and the one who passionately follows Christ will experience suffering as a result, for she will come into conflict, a "collision," with the patterns of the world. The world (including Christendom) may react to the one who acts in accordance with the divine command, to love the neighbor as herself, as they reacted to Jesus Christ.

As Kierkegaard transitioned toward his "attack upon Christendom," he increasingly spoke of Christianity (the essentially Christian, in contrast to Christendom) in terms of a direct confrontation—an offense—with the world. In a journal entry, he noted, "The characteristically Christian suffering is to suffer at the hands of men [sic]. This is consistent with the Christian view that to love God is to hate the world . . ."[16] In Denmark, Kierkegaard would say, there was no such thing as a "non-Christian," culturally speaking. Christendom had become "the world"; it had set itself against the essentially Christian. It is crucial to keep in mind that, in Kierkegaard's context, "the world" means Christendom.

---

12. *EUD*, 335.
13. *WL*, 138.
14. Ibid.
15. *WL*, 139.
16. *JP* 4, 4709.

In his two late essays, *For Self-Examination* and *Judge for Yourself!*, Kierkegaard spelled out the notion that Christian faith, which ventures to follow the narrow way of Christ defined by death on the cross and burial in the tomb, is a faith defined by "restlessness."[17] The cross is the end of the narrow way of death that includes poverty, abasement, and the radical imitation of Jesus' sufferings.[18] The cruciform life resists the flimsy spirit of the age, which is propped up weakly by the human spirit rather than by the Holy Spirit, whose gift of new life comes only "on the other side of [one's own] death."[19] Kierkegaard longed for the Holy Spirit to be the "coachman," giving people a true understanding of themselves and what it would mean for them to transform the world—and their own hearts.[20]

As he saw it, the challenge of recovering Christianity in the midst of Christendom was to reestablish what it means "to come to oneself in self-knowledge and before God as nothing before him, yet infinitely, unconditionally engaged."[21] This requires the recognition of an organic link between understanding and action. To know is to act. In turn, the action that responds in faith and gratitude probes further questions: "Where are we? What is the situation in Christendom?"[22] Kierkegaard was anxious to convince his readers that self-knowledge comes in (or even after) the moment of action. It is in acting toward truth that one comes to know, rightfully, what is true, thus avoiding the travesty of inebriated self-denial.[23] Christianity driven by and toward works of love resists "assurances" and seeks after "witnesses to the truth."[24] As Kierkegaard put it, the objectification of Christianity has abolished it:

> Christianity is an objective doctrine and it makes no difference how it is served; "the doctrine" is everything. It is this that has abolished Christianity. It is easy to understand. There is an existential qualification of the essentially Christian that is the unconditional

---

17. *FSE*, 17–23, 55–63.
18. *FSE*, 67–69.
19. *FSE*, 82.
20. *FSE*, 87.
21. *FSE*, 104.
22. *FSE*, 123, 129.
23. *FSE*, 121–22.
24. *FSE*, 125, 129.

condition: otherwise Christianity cannot be introduced. It is: to die to.[25]

For Kierkegaard, "what we called Christianity was not really Christianity at all; it was a very toned down conception, something distantly related to Christianity."[26] "Christ as prototype" is defined, in essence, by the way of the cross, the *cruciform* life: the cross signifies not superficiality or a "decoration, a cross in a medal." Rather, it means becoming nothing, diverting attention from yourself, suffering for the doctrine, humility, and discipleship: this is "the next kind of Christianity."[27] For Kierkegaard, "there is really only one true way to be a Christian—to be a disciple," which is to follow the prototype, the pattern, in Jesus Christ; this means *voluntary* suffering.[28] True Christianity has to be seen in light of its center in Christ, the "pattern" and "prototype"; the incarnate Christ must be the ideal. Yet, the consolation also remains: because we cannot consistently follow the ideal, we need grace. But grace is not a lessening of the ideal; rather, it is a divine gift that accompanies the difficult command. Both aspects must be retained. This understanding of Christianity as *following*, or imitating, the prototype, runs counter to the "age of reflection." It is the way of action, which gives rise to a "revolutionary" relationship to the world. This revolution is not violent but is spurred by authentic inwardness. It is the "sober" way of Jesus, to which we are called. It is the way of *works of love*.

Those who wish to have their Christianity admired by others are like the Pharisees, who wished to be seen praying and fasting in public. But for Kierkegaard, Christians who follow the way of the essentially Christian are not like actors in a theater who provide artistic enjoyment for others. The authentic Christian "performs" (if you can call it that) for God, not for others.[29] For Kierkegaard, the "language" by which we must address God is

---

25. *FSE*, 131.

26. *FSE*, 142.

27. *FSE*, 161, 174–75, 179, 189, 198, 203, 205.

28. *FSE*, 201.

29. *JP* 3, 3541. Kierkegaard similarly noted, "The medium in which you are a Christian has decisive significance for the Christian life. To be a Christian in the medium of imagination (hidden inwardness—the artistic pomp and ceremony on Sunday etc.) is playing at Christianity. To be a Christian in the world, which Christianity calls the evil, sinful world, this actual world—that is what is meant by being a Christian according to the New Testament. . . . God, who is himself actuality, wants this actual world to be the setting for being a Christian" (*JP* 3, 2359).

the language of action, not of abstraction or speculation, or in superficial "activities" deemed to be religious:

> God has a particular language for addressing him—it is action, the transformation of the mind, the expression in one's life; it is no good for us to bow and scrape before him in words and phrases and in such activities as building churches and binding Bibles in velvet.[30]

You might say that Kierkegaard, who was reintroducing James into Christendom, recognized that "true religion" is to "look after orphans and widows in their distress and to keep oneself from being polluted by the world" (Jas 1:27).

What is the consequence of Kierkegaard's notion that authentic Christian inwardness is by duty engaged in works of love? First, we see that Kierkegaard certainly had a place for the social outworking of authentic inwardness and religious subjectivity. The appropriation of Christian truth, the deepening of inwardness, and following Christ in the world means that there will be suffering ("collision" with the world) and transformations (even "social" transformations) that occur as a result. In short, a Kierkegaardian emphasis on works of love as the expression of authentic inwardness has built within it the possibility of profound, *restless* action and motivations for social justice and for prophetic, real-world witness. As one theologian notes,

> Kierkegaard's concentration on the impassioned appropriation of Christianity does not in any way exclude reforms, social development, participation in politics, a Christian social ethic, and so on, and the anarchist demand for destruction of all social forms is nowhere to be found. Instead, Kierkegaard fought against the—on his view—false value placed on the social. Reforms, societies, political participation—without individuals capable of making judgments—quickly deteriorate into mere power games played for group interests, into a caricature of the community as a whole.[31]

Nonetheless, Kierkegaard was acutely aware that *people*, not circumstances or reform of systems, can bring about transformation in the world by living out the essentially Christian. Of course, people must be empowered by the Holy Spirit—but they will be so empowered to the

30. *JP* 4, 4914.

31. Deuser, "Religious Dialectics and Christology," 395.

extent that they are following the narrow way of Christ. This way of following Christ, this disposition of subjectivity applied socially by works of love, will be an apologetic of witness rather than the witness of apologetics.

THE APOLOGETIC OF WITNESS

"The truth of Christianity is not established through any speculative calculus. Instead of being 'proven' it is testified to—by the one who lives it.... [W]hat is given in Jesus, as testified to in the New Testament, is simply to be proclaimed. It cannot be subjected to a proof."[32]

The notion that works of love are central to the authentic Christian life also raises the specter of the relation between the church and politics; it puts us into the sphere of political theology. As we have seen, against the modern emphasis on objectivity, Kierkegaard understood Christianity as an authentic—but not "hidden" (or *quietistic*)—inwardness, which involves unplugging from the dominant, often oppressive social order, standing before God, and reengaging the social order in light of the primacy of the God-relationship (God as "middle term"). This is not a form of subjective isolation from social concern; rather, it prophetically affords an opportunity for social and political critique, while exposing the unstable, transient nature of temporality. Charles Mathewes, though not writing about Kierkegaard, offers a sentiment that I think captures well the primacy of the God-relationship in the way that the Christian community relates to the political:

> So Christian faith, lived vigorously in community, keeps politics honest, because the eschatological dimensions of such faith oppose the apocalyptic dimensions of politics, which must inevitably move in the direction of false (that is, idolatrous) consciousness. Faith lets us see that there are no final solutions in politics, that there is no end to politics, not in this life.[33]

Mathewes argues that faith has a unique way of deconstructing politics when it becomes idolatrous and all-consuming, by keeping it "playful" and preventing "suffocation." As Kierkegaard would affirm, for the Christian and for the Christian community, the political is subordinate to the God-relationship and to the primacy and actuality of works of love. Nonetheless,

32. Rae, *Kierkegaard and Theology*, 60.
33. Mathewes, *Republic of Grace*, 206.

works of love take concrete, tangible shape in the world and have transformational power. But what is the nature of that tangible shape, in terms of the political and the social? Kierkegaard offers us little explicit direction.

This discussion raises a common—and understandable—critique that Kierkegaard's religious ethics were not specific enough. The irony is palpable, since Kierkegaard adamantly affirmed the importance of the specific, the particular, and the *actual*. David Law, discussing Kierkegaard's hermeneutics as it relates to the law, expresses a common frustration that he did not offer us much by way of tangible specificity, in terms of what obedience looks like in practical reality.[34] Kierkegaard was fond of expressing his distaste for the abstract. And yet, we find little by way of specific ethical direction in his reflections, particularly regarding complex social issues or challenging moral dilemmas. Should a Christian go to war? Should a Christian be a pacifist? Should a Christian serve in government? How should they spend their money? Which economic system is most just? How do we work toward human flourishing and the common good in a pluralistic society? How can we ensure that the Enlightenment quest for freedom and dignity of all peoples is fulfilled?

If we translate the question of specificity over from ethics to an apologetic of witness, we could ask the same question of Kierkegaard: that is, why the lack of concrete specificity? As we observed in our discussion of hermeneutics (chapter 3), Kierkegaard did not want to speak for God and did not want to interfere with the sacred specificity of the God-relationship. Moreover, the individual is not without guidance; rather, the individual is a part of a community of questers and interpreters. Furthermore, the individual has the interpretive help of the Holy Spirit. God speaks to the individual and yet simultaneously through the community, as each person individually and in community—in a dialectical, dialogical process in which all are attending to the activity and leading of the Spirit—seeks to act in accordance with divine love. In any case, Kierkegaard was less interested in setting forth a strategic, social agenda, ethical code, or political strategy than he was in getting to the root of the matter: the heart, or the inward disposition of the self before God. The understanding that the essentially Christian consists in love for God and love for neighbor is a good place to start. When the works of the Christian—as responses to God's grace—are focused on the crucified, paradoxical Christ, the tangible, concrete effects will reflect the rhythms of Jesus' ministry.

34. "Cheap Grace and the Cost of Discipleship," 135–36.

Emerging Prophet

Along with Kierkegaard's deconstruction of the idolatry of the "political," this inward stance before God also involves a critique of modernist discourse—particularly "classical apologetics," those forms of witness common to fundamentalist evangelicalism. Kierkegaard's apologetic of witness entails a shift from an objective emphasis on propositional precision and rational argument to a subjective, existential, and practical accent. Communication, under this shift, emphasizes *how* one witnesses as much (or more) than *what* is said (the objective). What matters most, in terms of the communication of Christian truth, is the life that is lived and the testimony rendered by that life. The doctrine, or the *what* (the material content), is communicated through the medium of the *how*. But the *how* is primary—and it involves action: not speculation, rational theologizing, or mere conceptual understanding. In other words, intellectual exercises can be a hindrance to the essentially Christian, since they so often are an excuse for passivity and for fending off the rigorousness to which the New Testament calls us. Furthermore, intellectual, apologetic exercises, which attempt to rationally "prove" Christianity, often only end up confirming the skeptic in his or her doubt.[35]

Kierkegaard argued that Christian truth must be communicated using an ironic, poetic, and postfoundationalist form of discourse he called *indirect communication*. This is because the recipients of the communication, "Christians" in Christendom, are deceived and deluded with respect to reality. Truth cannot be communicated directly to those who are fundamentally self-deceived. As we have seen, Kierkegaard used pseudonyms, parables, and a variety of points of view to enable his readers to engage imaginatively and authentically with their existential state—and thereby to be awakened to their self-deception. But Kierkegaard's central insight, which drove his imaginative authorship, is that Christianity "is not a doctrine" but an existence-communication. This bears out an implication for the communication of Christianity to outsiders: the best way to communicate Christianity is not by intellectual arguments but by imitators, or *followers*, of Christ. Existing in what one understands to be the truth ("living it out,"

---

35. C. Stephen Evans points out that Kierkegaard's primary critique of classical apologetics is that it underestimates the role of the *will* in religious belief. The problem is not so much intellectual as it is existential: "The problem may lie in our constricted understanding of what our essential task is as human beings and our impoverished attempts to become selves. It is not that we are too intelligent and learned to become Christians, but that we have deceived ourselves into thinking that intellectual achievements are what human life is all about." Evans, *Søren Kierkegaard's Christian Psychology*, 119.

Reclaiming Love

as we might say), or "reduplication," is the ideal of the communication of Christian truth.[36] For Kierkegaard, an authentic life lived "before God" and lived out through works of love is the most powerful apologetic witness to the truth. One cannot assume the epistemological right-of-way in a postmodern, postfoundational context. Those who suffer for the sake of the truth they proclaim offer a compelling testimony to its reality. Kierkegaard's approach to the communication of Christianity is a timely one for our increasingly pluralistic society: people—and communities—who attempt to embody Christ's cruciform narrative and to practice works of love in the world are his most effective witnesses. Emergent Christianity seems to be deeply receptive to this shift and convinced that the best apologetic approach in our day, or the most effective communication of the essentially Christian, is an authentic faith—a cruciform life lived in community on behalf of others.

THE WITNESS OF LOVE AND WORKS OF LOVE

"The witness of the church is its life. The question of authentic witness is the question of authentic community."[37]

The theme of witness, or testimony, is both thoroughly biblical and a timely metaphor for the task of communicating Christianity in our postmodern world.[38] Witness must be understood with reference to its ground in love. There is no better witness to the essentially Christian than works of love performed by Christians in community. Ray Anderson, in *An Emergent Theology for Emerging Churches*, suggests that an emergent theology advocates a "law of love" over the "letter of the law." To be human is to need love: "Love is the single criterion for that which upholds the dignity, integrity, and essential value of the other person in the concreteness of every social relation and every culture."[39] God's commandments ("love your neighbor as yourself"; "owe no one anything except to love!") take into account the fundamental human need to be loved and seek to ensure the primacy of

---

36. *JP* 1, 484.
37. Kraus, *Authentic Witness*, 156.
38. See also Richard Bauckham's *Bible and Mission*, which develops this argument from the perspective of biblical theology.
39. Anderson, *Emergent Theology*, 142.

love as motivating Christian action. Genuine Christian love, which follows the pattern of Jesus, refuses to reduce genuine love into either patronizing sentiment or triumphalist proselytizing. True love respects the sacredness of the "other": "In the real humanity of Jesus we see the humanization as well as the socialization of humanity."[40]

Divine love does not share the motivations common to political revolutions, but is impelled by the deeper, more human, more Christlike understanding of love as—to use Kierkegaard's term again—genuine inwardness. This kind of love enables "a reciprocity of relations in which Jesus Christ is present as the objective reality of grace, freedom, and responsibility."[41] Love does not change with the tides of culture, but remains an enduring, permanent force regardless of external circumstances. Society is *humanized* by the presence of divine love.

In another work, Anderson argues, "ethical norms remain constant when grounded in the true humanity of the other person rather than in culturally conditioned self-perceptions of individuals or the collective cultural mass."[42] Ideological commitments, he asserts, fall to the wayside in the light of the action of love, which affirms the "true humanity" of all persons: "The moral good of the other person constitutes an ethical criterion from which no one is exempt by virtue of doctrinal, ideological, ecclesiological, or political commitments."[43] The recognition of the *imago Dei* in every human being grounds human morality in an unflinching, irrepressible respect for the other. This relational and theological approach is far from the "relativism" with which postmodernity is so often associated. We might say, referring to Caputo and Derrida, that love—along with justice—is "un-deconstructible." This is not the same as setting up a universal system of abstract moral principles (it does not collapse into *moralism*), because love is "always acting in a concrete situation where one becomes the neighbor of the other."[44] The relationality of love becomes a *rationality* of love: communities that operate on the basis of the primacy of love discover their criterion for action in the particularity of those relational contexts. What is a "loving" action? Specific responses to the question cannot be circumscribed in a universal way by law—at least not in a way impervious to

40. Ibid., 143.
41. Ibid., 145.
42. Anderson, *Shape of Practical Theology*, 174.
43. Ibid., 151.
44. Anderson, *Emergent Theology*, 148.

deconstruction, as times, situations, and people change. Love and justice are twin "good ghosts" who permeate the flux of history with a transcendent pulse. If any principle can be said to have universal status in Christian theology (along with the doctrine of the Trinity), it is the *imago Dei* and the great commandment to love God and neighbor as oneself.

John Caputo, in his discussion of Derrida, notes that deconstruction is ultimately about love: it "does not take a single step without love."[45] Deconstruction is the "affirmation of the impossible"; it is the unanticipatable anticipation of the "event," which cannot be grasped, owned, or mastered.[46] Love is to "surrender to the impossible."[47] Caputo likens Derrida's notion of love to the *apophatic* tradition of theology, which attempts to say the unsayable only by saying what it is not. That is, the apophatic tradition recognizes that the object of knowledge must be respected as ultimately mysterious: it cannot be mastered, but it can be experienced. It can be worshipped. But that is precisely the point: to love is to love in the actual—even if the actual is mysterious. Caputo says, "What would love or justice or hospitality require, here and now, in the concrete?"[48] There can be no clear-cut criteria for determining what love is (no abstract principles). One has to attain to the "spirit" of deconstruction's understanding of love: "a spirit of prayers and tears, of madness and excess, for justice and the gift . . ." The ultimate expression of the apophatic nature of love, Caputo suggests, can be seen in what he calls the "theo-poetics of the kingdom" of God.[49] To love, with the kind of love that resists deconstruction, is to engage in a paradoxical reality:

> The key to the kingdom is to love those who do not love you, who hate you, and whom you, by worldly standards, should also hate. That is exactly the madness that a deconstructive analysis of love would predict. Loving the lovable is entirely possible, but loving the unlovable, those who are impossible to love, that is when the kingdom reigns. Loving the unlovable, the possibility of the impossible, that is the central symmetry that leads me to treat deconstruction as the hermeneutics of the kingdom of God.[50]

---

45. Caputo, *What Would Jesus Deconstruct?*, 78.
46. Ibid.
47. Ibid., 80.
48. Ibid.
49. Ibid., 81.
50. Ibid., 84.

Emerging Prophet

THE APOLOGETIC OF WITNESS IS A COMMUNITY OF LOVE

As the social outworking of authentic subjectivity, the witness of love is the best hope for society's transformation. The community of love is an apologetic of witness. In a book that was a lightning rod for the contemporary missional church movement, Darrell Guder wrote:

> Not isolated individuals but a redeemed people who are experiencing reconciliation with God and fellowship with each other is called to witness to God's intent to overcome the rebellion and alienation of humanity through the establishment of a new society of joy, righteousness, faith, and love. Salvation is not a private transaction between the individual and God, but a social reality of transformed relationships. The cultivating of missional communities through ecclesial practices is not simply an instrumental means to a desired end, but manifests itself in the very mission of the church: "the life of the church *is* its witness. The witness of the church *is* its life. The question of authentic witness is the question of authentic community."[51]

Walter Brueggemann, reflecting on the church's prospects for taking on a constructive role in society, referenced Robert Bellah's analysis of contemporary American life, which Bellah characterizes by the terms "positivism, reductionism, relativism, and determinism."[52] The culture of the United States suffers from the transformation of a formally visible (and locally integrated) social and economic life. We are now "a society vastly more interrelated and integrated economically, technically, and functionally." Yet this transformation has meant a loss of shared meanings and a lack of common understanding.[53] Bellah argues that religious communities offer the best antidote to the dehumanizing ("antihuman") structures of modern culture. They can be "demonstration communities," or in Brueggemann's words, "communities of obedience," that preserve "elementary decencies" through the passage of time and culture.[54]

---

51. Guder, *Missional Church*, 182. The embedded quotation is from Kraus, *Authentic Witness*, 156.

52. Brueggemann, *Book that Breathes New Life*, 6.

53. Bellah et al., *Habits of the Heart*, 50.

54. Bellah, "Biblical Religion and Social Science in the Modern World," 21–22, cited in Brueggemann, *Book that Breathes New Life*, 6–7. As Brueggemann puts it: "The test in this time of need for human possibility is in praxis, that is, in the emergence of communities that embody and implement the rereading of the world which is voiced in the text. These communities of obedience bear witness to the authorizing power of the book

In other words, the church offers society a revaluation of meanings and a reintegration of the disparate, disconnected elements of the human experience.[55] Christian communities, to the extent that they are comprised of authentic questers who seek to embody the gospel, to follow Christ in the world, and to perform works of love as they interact with the cultural, social, and religious "other," create spaces within society that demonstrate the love of God and that press against the grain of society's tendency to forget the powerless and vulnerable. Christian communities should understand that proclamation of the gospel involves an embodiment of the gospel (or at least the *attempt* at embodiment) and that the church's best witness today is through a holistic application of inwardness in the direction of the "social." Richard Rubenstein suggests that

> The call for religious transformation is in reality a call to conversion, a call to change ourselves. Our preachers have rightly told us that we must be converted, that we must be born again. Unfortunately, what has been understood as conversion has all too often been devoid of the inclusive social component our times demand. In truth, we must be born again as men and women blessed with the capacity to care for each other here and now.[56]

The emphasis on church as witness implies that the ultimate purposes of the church have little or nothing to do with the church's self-preservation as a religious institution; instead, they have everything to do with "God's redemptive purposes in the world."[57] Christians—and the church as the community of Christians gathered for worship and scattered for witness—have as their driving goal the expression of God's love in the world through action.

I will address the nature and vocation of the church more thoroughly in the following chapter; suffice it now to say that Kierkegaard's emphasis on works of love as the social outworking of the essentially Christian offers a powerful theological grounding for not only an emergent apologetic of witness, but also an emergent ecclesiology of love. Furthermore, this prioritizing of love seems fundamental to the ethos of emergent Christianity. For emergent Christians, the best (or only?) way to practice divine love is in

---

as well as to the spirit that blows through that book." *Book that Breathes New Life*, 15.

55. Brueggemann, *Book that Breathes New Life*, 6–7

56. Rubenstein, *Age of Triage*, 240, cited in Brueggemann, *Book that Breathes New Life*, 7.

57. Hays, "Ecclesiology and Ethics," 5.

and through a holistic, inclusive community. This conviction is articulated well in the book *Emerging Churches*:

> Emerging churches raise basic questions about the nature of church. Is it the place where weekly worship services are conducted, or is it a network of relationships? Emerging churches utilize the gospel both to dismantle and to rebuild church forms, marking a significant shift of emphasis from church to kingdom. The practice of inclusion creates a new kind of family. "Who is my mother, and who are my brothers?" Jesus asked his followers (Matt 12:48 NIV). Jesus turned the family structure on its head. Yes, the followers of Jesus lived as family, but this new family was not connected by blood relations. Those who pursued the kingdom served as brother and sister to one another.[58]

When the church, the people of God, is impelled by divine love, it understands itself as an instantiation of the kingdom. This kingdom is organized by a gift economy rather than an exchange of goods and services (*this* for *that*). Kester Brewin, in *Signs of Emergence*, suggests that because Christ modeled this free-flowing gift economy, the emergent church ought to be a "center of gift exchange." It should be "the empty-handed church, happy to receive gifts and pass them on into mystery, refusing to hold on to them for our own blessing."[59] Our greatest example of this, Brewin says, is Christ, who "crawled out of the desert" of temptation to give the ultimate gift—the gift of life and the gift of his life for the world.[60] So the church should be motivated by Christ's example, understanding its vocation in the world to be givers of gifts.

Peter Rollins asks us to reflect on the "new mode of being" that is opened up by the radical nature of the Christ-event.[61] This event challenges, even impels, the church to "expose the hegemonic ideology of the day as *contingent* and thus to provide the possibility of creating substantive societal change . . ."[62] Conformity to the mind of Christ allows for an unplugging from the "ideologies of the world," which catalyzes the imagination to "imagine and implement radical alternatives that help to

---

58. Gibbs and Bolger, *Emerging Churches*, 97.
59. Brewin, *Signs of Emergence*, 163.
60. Ibid.
61. Rollins, "Worldly Theology of Emerging Christianity," 25.
62. Ibid.

bring substantive, though no less contingent, change to society."[63] Rollins calls the consequences of embracing the transformation wrought by the Christ-event a "moment of participating in *kenosis*," whereby members of the community participate as servants to each other and as servant (rather than lord or ruler) to the greater society.[64]

The orientation around love as the supreme value has implications for how the community relates not only to those on the "outside" (the "non-Christian"), but also to those on the inside. In short, emergent communities that aspire to reflect the apologetic of witness to the world should assume a posture of deference, or *kenosis*, to the outsider as well as a posture of inclusive embrace of the insider. This means that regardless of personal identity markers, which are transient and given to the flux and flow of temporality, every person—created in the image of God—is deserving of absolute respect and is equal partner to and recipient of the gift of divine love. One implication of this is a deeply ecumenical approach to Christian worship and practice. McLaren, in discussing the present and future of the emerging church, asks: "What if our churches abolished categories and labels such as 'Baptist,' 'Presbyterian,' 'Catholic,' etc., and instead thought of themselves as training centers of love?"[65] Similarly, in *A New Kind of Christianity*, he suggests that, in the Apostle Paul's mind, the church "must be above all a school of love."[66] The church is not primarily an intellectual center or a dispenser of information, but "a community where you see living examples of Christlikeness and experience inner formation."[67] McLaren here captures the centrality of love as an orientation toward God and toward the "other." This notion is similar to what Tony Jones suggests as a primary metaphor for the emerging church:

> Everything we do in the emergent church is surrounded by an envelope of friendship, friendship that is based on lives of reconciliation. And it's within that envelope that we have all sorts of discussions and debates about the atonement and sex trafficking and baptism and AIDS in Africa.[68]

Likewise, Karen Ward proposes that the church's theology is to be driven by a "communal response to and reflection upon God's invitation

63. Ibid.
64. Ibid.
65. From the DVD that accompanies McKnight et al., *Church in the Present Tense*.
66. McLaren, *New Kind of Christianity*, 170.
67. Ibid.
68. Jones, *New Christians*, 78.

and pursuit of love."⁶⁹ The local, gathered Christian community is "firstly a community of 'God-beloved lovers of God,'" which means that theological reflection is subordinate to "pursuits to our love of God."⁷⁰ In Kierkegaardian fashion, once again, emergent Christianity reflects the priority of tangible action and the secondary (though still significant) nature of "reflection"—even of the theological. She sums up her vision of the church as a community of love, giving out invitations by "introducing love to Love" and leaving entrance into the kingdom up to God.⁷¹

Kierkegaard, as an emerging prophet, pushes us toward a definition of the vision of the Christian life as works of love. This reveals much synergy with the express, central values of the emergent church. To be a community that follows after Christ is to voluntarily look beyond the "otherness" of those within and those without, affirming the sacredness of the *imago Dei* and the centrality of works of love in the Christian life. This does not discount the reality of sin or undermine its seriousness. Choices still need to be made regarding what counts as legitimate expressions of Christian faith and what will make for authentic, vibrant, individual and communal lives. Nonetheless, differences in religion, sexual identity, ethnicity, economic and social status, etc., cannot determine the value of a person in the eyes of God—and thereby in the Christian community called "church." In other words, if we are going to practice works of love, we will need to get over our fear of otherness and overcome our tendency to universalize, in a dogmatic and triumphalist way, our contextually located convictions. This does not mean that we set aside discussions of sin, justice, and holiness. Christians will disagree on these matters of conviction. But disagreements ought not to threaten the universality of the *imago Dei*, nor should they undermine the positive force of love and justice. The question I am pushing for here is this: what happens if (or when) love of God and of neighbor, as patterned after Christ, becomes the primary, motivating factor in our relational lives and in our Christian communities? Can a value be placed on that? Can rules or principles be set in stone that capture that mysterious reality and that serve as a guide for others? Certainly the Decalogue was "set in stone" and has persisted over time within Judeo-Christianity as an organizing motif for our ethical, moral, and religious lives. And yet the commandments too, Jesus told us, were "completed" in and through the person of Jesus.

69. Ward, "Emerging Church and Embodied Theology," 163.
70. Ibid.
71. Ibid.

"This is the first and only commandment," he said—to love God and love neighbor. Everything is summed up in love—especially in works of love.

Conclusion

The essentially Christian is defined by the centrality of divine love and culminates in works of love. The Christian who engages life as a quest for existential authenticity and the appropriation of Christian truth, by following Christ down the narrow path, organizes one's life around a central concern: the concern regarding whether or not his or her actions are works of love. Placing love as the central value does not mean the abdication of particularity or the minimizing of difference. Nor does it mean that prophetic action is neglected in favor of sentimental feeling or unconditional acceptance of sin or tolerance of injustice and oppression. When love is primary, justice will be pursued and righteousness will be longed for. Christians, who act in accordance with divine love, carry on in the spirit and mission of Jesus, following him in the way of suffering, of self-sacrifice, and of love for the "other." Emergent Christians already recognize the value of diversity and difference (even though their actual communities are not immune to homogeneity) because they recognize that, epistemologically and otherwise, they have no upper hand. There should be no such thing. They are well positioned to act together as "demonstration communities," or "communities of obedience," testifying to the primacy of God's love. This recognition means that ecclesiology, in the emerging church, looks different than in much of traditional, institutional religion. It means that the way the emerging church understands its identity and vocation in the world stands in contrast—perhaps even starkly so—to the organizations and values of Christendom. The question then remains: what shape might the church, the postmodern people of God, take when it is organized around the centrality of works of love and when it sees its vocation in the world as an apologetic of witness? In the following chapter, we explore in more detail the relation between Kierkegaard's reflections on Christian community and the understanding of emergent leaders of the shape and vocation of the postmodern people of God.

Chapter Six

AGAINST CHRISTENDOM

"Every hour that this order of things stands, the crime is continued; every Sunday divine worship service is conducted in this way, Christianity is made a game and a fool is made of God. Everyone who participates is participating in playing at Christianity and in making a fool of God, is involved in the Christian criminal case."[1]

IN "METAMORPHOSIS: FROM CHRISTENDOM to Diaspora," theologian Douglas John Hall argued that Western Christianity in the late modern period is being slowly and painfully weaned from the triumphalism, elitism, and unhealthy conflation of Christian discipleship with the cultural and social power that marked the church of modernity. Hall's message to the churches is this: "Go ahead and finish the job—disestablish yourselves."[2] This chapter follows in the spirit of Hall's challenge, offering up Kierkegaard as a resource for the intentional, *theologically empowered* disestablishment of Western Christianity (Christendom). While Hall's essay, published more than a decade ago, was directed primarily toward the mainline Lutheran church in North America, the message is no less relevant for evangelical Christianity today. Its relevance holds for all modernist forms of Christianity, whether liberal or conservative. This chapter points to glimmers

---

1. *TM*, 168.
2. Hall, "Metamorphosis."

Against Christendom

of hope for a "disestablished church" in emergent Christianity—a church beyond the modernist impasse. The point of contact between these ecclesiological experiments and Kierkegaard's disestablishment lies in a robust Christology. The final section of the chapter will explore areas of overlap with Kierkegaard's disestablishment and emergent Christianity, in particular the philosophy of deconstruction that inspires much of the emergent movement.

Naturally, this chapter marks the climax of the argument of this book: Kierkegaard's understanding of divine revelation, his chastened epistemology and relational view of truth (subjectivity), his "apologetic of witness" and emphasis on works of love, and his christocentric theology of discipleship all lead into a renewed vision for the identity and vocation of the church. For Kierkegaard, Christendom requires radical deconstruction in order to remove the idols that stand in the way of the essentially Christian. Indeed, Kierkegaard's most pointed relevance today may be as a prophetic voice for the Christian church in America. This seems appropriate because the established, institutional church was the target of Kierkegaard's criticism, in his notorious "attack upon Christendom," during the final years of his life (1854–55). He targeted—with a spirited relentlessness—the gatekeepers of institutional Christianity: bishops, pastors, and theologians. Kierkegaard wondered: if Jesus were to walk into a church today, would he recognize it as consistent with the New Testament? Kierkegaard thought not. He bluntly proclaimed that, in Denmark, "Christianity does not exist at all."[3] Indeed, Christianity had become something altogether different from what Jesus had initiated, as expressed in the New Testament.

Emergent Christianity is attempting to navigate the thorny terrain opened up by a strange, new world—a world in which, while established Christianity is still thriving in pockets across the country, its future seems precarious. Might emergent Christianity, as one instantiation of a broader renewal movement (what Phyllis Tickle calls "Emergence Christianity"), have an important role to play in navigating that terrain?[4] If so, Kierkegaard offers theological guidance and a timely prophetic voice for that task. While there are clear resonances between Kierkegaard's critical ecclesiology and the ethos of emergent Christianity, there are also prophetic warnings.

---

3. *JP* 3, 2915.
4. See Tickle, *Emergence Christianity*.

THE PROBLEM WITH CHRISTENDOM: OUR PRESENT *KAIROS* MOMENT

Kierkegaard was convinced that the message of the Gospels and the way of life to which Christ called his followers—a life marked by suffering, self-denial, and love—had been turned into a culturally and institutionally encumbered religion that sanctions materialism, justifies religious careerism, and that substituted genuine religious faith for nationalistic fervor (the "sepulchers of the prophets" and the garnished "tombs of the righteous"). Kierkegaard claimed that, above all, he simply wanted a public admission by its institutional leaders that the Christianity of the New Testament no longer existed in Denmark.

Kierkegaard's theology of the self and his understanding of subjectivity can function as a critique of the tendencies toward idolatry and institutionalization latent in modernist forms of religion. Calvin Schrag has insightfully suggested that Kierkegaard's "religiousness A" (the sphere of immanent, "pagan" religiosity) could be added to Kant's three culture-spheres of modernity: morality, art, and science. The addition of religiousness A would provide a greater understanding of the varied features of modernity.[5] Religion (as "religiousness A") would then constitute a given culture's institutional expressions, articulations, and experiences of the divine—replete with established patterns, values, and practices that make up a given society's religious forms and practices. "Religiousness B," on the other hand, is an existential and critical impulse rather than a culture-sphere or an institutional religion. It is not defined by "adhering to the doctrines and practices of a particular religion"; thus it "provides the measure against the recurring idolatric tendencies across the spectrum of culture-spheres."[6] Against the tendency of modernists to "make hegemonic claims for ultimacy" (whether in the realm of morality, art, science, or religion), Schrag suggests that religiousness B "can be understood as a 'critical principle,' a principle of protest" that "needs to be used against religion itself."[7]

New Testament Christianity, Kierkegaard insisted, is not meant to provide a safe haven from existential doubt and suffering or from the responsibility to safeguard the value of all people. Furthermore, it was not meant to provide people with a sense of mastery over the world or a sense

---

5. Schrag, "Kierkegaard-Effect."
6. Ibid., 12.
7. Ibid., 12–13.

that humanity has "arrived" by virtue of participating in a particular religious framework. The framework of the Christian religion can be a medium through or under which people experience God—in particular the God of Jesus Christ. When a person is properly related to God, however, the "externals" that make up the framework are always open to critique. The idols and ideologies perpetuated by the framework are always (or should always be) a target for deconstruction.

Elements of American Christianity still resemble the situation of Kierkegaard's Christendom. It may seem cliché, but the temptations toward consumerism, triumphalism, ideological colonialism, nationalism, and cultural Christianity are still with us; they still confound the mission of the church and can still lead to a confusion of the meaning of the gospel. Furthermore, a consensus is emerging: the American church has reached a tipping point toward numerical decline and a loss of social influence. Diana Butler Bass, in her book *Christianity After Religion,* summarizes much of the available sociological data regarding the trajectories of Christianity and argues persuasively that the decline of American Christianity, in its heavily "institutionalized" manifestations, must be taken seriously. In this time of present and coming fissure, she suggests that a new opportunity is emerging for rethinking the nature of established, institutional Christianity and for embracing a new "spiritual awakening."[8] The church may be entering a *kairos* moment, an opportunity to rethink its purpose and the ways in which it will carry out its purpose in the world. It has been graced with the chance to, as Hall suggested, "disestablish itself" and to theologically reimagine its existence in ways that might be more consistent with the vision of the New Testament.[9] This rethinking can be painful and may require great sacrifices. It will certainly invite some new challenges. But it will also create new opportunities for capturing a fresh, powerful vision for testifying to the gospel. Emergent Christianity is an important movement in this *kairos* moment. It is not the only answer and is certainly not the only response, but it is a significant critical, creative, and imaginative renewal impulse that merits attention.

---

8. Bass, *Christianity After Religion,* 35.
9. Hall, "Metamorphosis," 76–77.

Defining "Disestablishment"

What might it mean, then, to disestablish Christianity? For Kierkegaard, established Christianity, or Christendom, carries in the first place the specific connotation of the conflation of the political and the religious, or the state and church, in Denmark. But it was not merely the governmental sanction and funding of the church that troubled him. Rather, established Christianity signified an array of negative consequences due, ultimately, to the Constantinization of the church. The church had become identified with a set of cultural practices and norms barely distinguishable from the world, which stood in stark contrast to New Testament Christianity. The primary consequence of the establishment of Christianity, for Kierkegaard, was the ease with which one "became" a Christian and the material and social achievement one stood to gain by it. *Christendom* was another term for the systemic propagation of a social, political, and cultural empire in which all are Christians as a matter of course and in which pastors and church officials stood to make a comfortable living on the death and resurrection of Christ.[10]

Kierkegaard's understanding of established Christendom can best be clarified by reference to the pseudonym Anti-Climacus' discussion of the "church triumphant" and the "church militant" in *Practice in Christianity*.[11] The church triumphant is comfortable in the world because it believes it represents the full arrival of God's kingdom. It relies on the grace of God and the finished work of Christ as a "result" that can now simply be appropriated without struggle. There is no process of *becoming* Christian; all are Christians as a matter of course. The church militant, by contrast, struggles to "make room for itself to exist."[12]

The key difference between the church triumphant and the church militant lies in their respective Christologies. The church militant

---

10. "It should not and must not be the highest and most earnest aim to get a secure position in the state church and make a living. . . . This business about going along with the established order of things, getting a secure position—all of which may be all right—if this is going to be life's highest earnestness, then Christ, the apostles, all Christians in the strictest sense of the word—are impractical visionaries" (JP 3, 376).

11. PC, 201–32. *Practice in Christianity* was Kierkegaard's attempt to "reintroduce Christianity into Christendom" by uplifting the high ideal of the New Testament and requesting a simple "admission" by the leadership of the establishment that they fell far short of the ideal—and needed God's grace and forgiveness. See the historical introduction to PC, xiv.

12. PC, 201.

recognizes the heterogeneity of the paradoxical God-man with the world. Christ is fundamentally different from human beings, and yet, paradoxically, he invites them to follow him in *imitation*. As Anti-Climacus put it, "Christ has never wanted to be victorious in this world. He came into the world in order to suffer; *that* he called being victorious."[13] Christ came proclaiming the kingdom of God; wherever the kingdom is equated with the world, "Christianity is abolished." Participation in the kingdom requires *conforming to the prototype* and suffering thereby.

The church militant consists of persons who rigorously follow in the way of the suffering, crucified Christ. The church is a kind of eschatological "parenthesis," which testifies to the abased, suffering Christ between the times of the ascension and coming *parousia*.[14] Living in the "parenthesis" means that Christ, heterogeneous with fallen humanity, cannot be accessed by humanity through objective means, but only by subjective appropriation. Christ can be believed, worshipped, and followed only in humble, active faith. The church triumphant views truth as propositional, didactic, and objective and relates to truth—and to Jesus—objectively. It believes that it has attained not only true Christianity, but also a final understanding of truth. The church militant, on the other hand, lives in a parenthetical, eschatological tension in which it never fully arrives and never finally becomes "Christian." In other words, it represents the New Testament notion that Christianity is a way, a process, a following of the paradoxical God-man within the messiness of temporal history. The tensions involved in following Christ will persist until the eschatological consummation of the kingdom of God.

For Kierkegaard, prior to 1854–55, the key to the disestablishment of the church lay not in altering its governance or polity nor in severing the relationship between the church and the state (e.g., advocating a "free church"), but in recovering a true inwardness marked by suffering, repentance, prayer, and genuine praxis.[15] Attempting to reform Christendom via an external, systemic solution would be yet another capitulation to secular-

---

13. *PC*, 224.

14. Kierkegaard's Anti-Climacus states, "Therefore, if I dare to put it this way, this form of existence makes the Church's whole existence here upon earth into a parenthesis or something parenthetical in Christ's life; the content of the parenthesis begins with Christ's ascension on high and ends with his coming again" (*PC*, 202).

15. "Let us not then—in order to divert!—convene synods or—in order to gain postponement!—appoint commissions. No, if something like this is to be done, then let a universal day of repentance and prayer be prescribed" (*Pap.* XI3 B 32).

ism; it would be to rely on "worldly" methods. However, by the time of his critical writings that comprise the collection titled *The Moment*, he had arrived at the conclusion that Christendom's state-church structure was beyond salvaging. If not even an admission could be made that the Christianity of Denmark did not match the ideals of the New Testament, then all hope was lost. In a preface to a new (1855) edition of *Practice in Christianity*, Kierkegaard noted that in the earlier edition he had incorrectly believed that Christendom could be reformed from within, via an admission of its failure to live up to the New Testament and a subsequent reliance on grace: "Now, however, I have completely made up my mind on two things: both that the established order is Christianly indefensible, that every day it lasts it is Christianly a crime; and that in this way one does not have the right to draw on grace."[16] Kierkegaard was finally convinced that the establishment had to be disestablished. But what would this imply about the nature and role of the church within Christianity and society? And what is the nature of Kierkegaard's disestablishment for our contemporary situation? In short, why does Kierkegaard still matter for how we understand the community of God?

Anti-Ecclesiology or Kenotic-Ecclesiology?

In *The Legacy of Kierkegaard*, Heywood Thomas asks whether Kierkegaard had "any notion of a church." He points to an 1854 newspaper article written by Kierkegaard's former theology professor and adversary in his *Attack upon Christendom*, the Hegelian minister Hans Martensen, who pronounced that "Dr. Kierkegaard's Christianity is without church and without history."[17] This claim sets the stage for a discussion about Kierkegaard's ecclesiology—or lack thereof. In this vein, David Law dubbed Kierkegaard's critique of established Christianity in his later years an "anti-ecclesiology."[18] He describes the stages through which his view of the "establishment" shifted and shows how his earlier patience with the state-church structure gave way eventually to a complete rejection of any role for the church in the task of imitating Christ and in following the imperatives of the New Testament.

16. *TM*, 70.

17. Martensen, *Berlingske Tidende*, cited in Heywood Thomas, *Legacy of Kierkegaard*, 137–38.

18. Law, "Kierkegaard's Anti-Ecclesiology."

I want to suggest, however, that Kierkegaard's "anti-ecclesiology" might be better understood as a *kenotic* ecclesiology, which was theologically derived from and dependent upon his Christology. If the church is to follow Christ in the world, the church must empty itself of its privilege, power, and materialism, and extricate itself from the conflation of church with cultural power and politics. Kierkegaard was finally pressing toward (albeit negatively) an understanding of the implications of a radical New Testament Christology for the idea of Christian life and community. One could argue that his distaste for the establishment corresponded with intuitions consistent with his early pietistic religious formation. For the early Pietists, the New Testament church was understood to be vitally present wherever communities of Christians could sustain a resistant, ambivalent, and even "militant" (to use Kierkegaard's term) relation to prevailing culture and worldly powers. It may be, then, that Kierkegaard's critique does not reflect an "anti-ecclesiology" so much as a radical ecclesiological alternative in which practices and values are derived from a robust Christology of the cross and are legitimated with respect to a dialectical encounter with the New Testament as governing text. For Kierkegaard, the disestablishment of the church was a necessary condition for the reappearance of Christ and the emergence of the kingdom of God in the world.

Kierkegaard's *Attack* was the result of his conviction that the New Testament church is not an established, static "culture" that can be subsumed by or immanently correlated to "the world." The genuine, suffering church always exists in a tension with worldly powers and concerns and must heed the voice of Christ calling it forward. The genuine church exists as a transient, instrumental reality that testifies to a truth that is deeper than its symbols, greater than its sacraments, and more powerful and prophetic than its institutions. For the suffering church, weakness is a value. As MacKinnon notes, only because of the fading of the Constantinian dream can Christianity recover the insight that the gospel is only truly displayed and communicated in "genuine weakness."[19] Kierkegaard advocates for a community of faithful, self-critical followers of Jesus who are willing to "suffer for the truth"; the vibrancy of these communities depends upon the passion and authenticity of the individual members' relation to God, to each other, and to the world. Heywood Thomas, answering his own question about whether Kierkegaard's Christianity has a place for the church, points out that an interpretation of Kierkegaard that claims he has no posi-

---

19. MacKinnon, *Stripping of the Altars*, 34, 39.

tive role for the church "reads the polemics undialectically."[20] Kierkegaard's position is a "dialectical" affirmation of the importance of ecclesiology with a corresponding acknowledgment that the existence of the church requires individual inwardness and subjectivity. Heywood Thomas is right when he says that when Kierkegaard attacked Christianity, he was really defending it.[21] Sometimes, as any good prophet will admit, the wounding *is* the healing.

EMERGING WEAKNESS: OR, WHAT WOULD KIERKEGAARD DECONSTRUCT?

In his conclusion, Law argued that although Denmark had become so thoroughly Christianized that Kierkegaard's strident criticisms of and eventual departure from the established church were understandable, the contemporary situation in Europe is sufficiently different from nineteenth-century Denmark to merit only a limited appropriation of the *Attack*. Europe's post-Christian climate reveals less a dogmatic triumphalism than an apathetic indifference toward Christianity. As I noted earlier, while Law's description of contemporary Europe is likely accurate, American Christianity, in many ways, still resembles the situation of Kierkegaard's Christendom. It is, in fact, this ethos against which many younger, postmodern-oriented Christians are reacting. Many are dissatisfied with what has been perceived as a long-standing confusion of Christianity with American consumerism, triumphalism, ideological colonialism, and nationalism.

Kierkegaard's call for the disestablishment of Christianity resonates with the longing of emergent thinkers for ecclesial renewal, for greater authenticity and openness to truth, for a post-Constantinian, postcolonial, and postconsumerist church. Like Kierkegaard, emergent Christians seem to want to escape the "crowd" and to discover a more theologically robust, inward, and quest-oriented faith. They express a readiness to deconstruct doctrines—or articulations of doctrines—that may no longer seem contextually relevant. Much of emergent Christianity seems to be pursuing something like Douglas John's Hall's vision for a *theologically* empowered, intentional disestablishment of the church.[22] In short, emerging Christians

20. Heywood Thomas, *Legacy of Kierkegaard*, 138.
21. Ibid., 139.
22. These communities have emerged in large part as an alternative to traditional, pragmatic, seeker-sensitive churches (e.g., Willow Creek), on the one hand, and to

generally advocate for a disestablishment from triumphalistic, pragmatic, or fundamentalist expressions of Christianity. They are pursuing a "new kind of Christianity" characterized by community, intellectual honesty, openness to doubt, emphasis on praxis, and desire for authenticity.[23]

The disestablishment of Christianity intimated in emergent Christianity is logically tied to the postmodern notion of deconstruction. The convergence of Kierkegaard's disestablishment with the tenor of emergent theology can perhaps best be conveyed through John Caputo's question, "What would Jesus deconstruct?" Another way of putting the question might be, What would happen if the Christian church became intensely concerned with Jesus' own eschatological message of the emerging kingdom of God? Deconstruction is a "work of love" and, for Caputo, "a hermeneutics of the kingdom of God."[24] Jesus appears as the "other" in the church and not as "one of us." The biblical Jesus is a stranger to institutional Christianity. He is excluded by those churches that adopt secular power models that, however "unintentionally," background or marginalize the "other," with whom and for whom Jesus exists. Some institutional churches, which neglect their first love, end up existing primarily for the purpose of self-preservation, sustaining their self-perpetuating ideologies, securing their material comfort, and justifying their personal satisfaction. So Caputo's question is a profoundly important one:

> So if we ask, "What would Jesus deconstruct?" the answer is first and foremost the church! For the idea behind the church is to give way to the kingdom, to proclaim and enact and finally disappear

---

conservative, fundamentalist churches, on the other hand, in which orthodoxy is prized over orthopraxy.

23. *A New Kind of Christianity* is the title of one of Brian McLaren's recent books. McLaren, the foremost representative of the emergent church, suggests that "Jesus didn't come to start a new religion, . . . he came to announce a new kingdom" (139). He came to invite people to follow in his path and announced the creation of a new way of living—the "kingdom of God." All could be citizens of this *"new kingdom,* the peaceable kingdom imagined by the prophets and inaugurated in Christ, learning its ways (as a disciple) and demonstrating in word and deed its presence and availability to all (as an apostle)" (140). The role of the church, in relation to the kingdom, is simply to create a space in which the Spirit can *"form Christlike people, people of Christlike love . . ."* (164). He suggest that, wherever this is happening, and in whatever denominational structure it occurs, "church is happening . . ." (171).

24. Caputo, *What Would Jesus Deconstruct?*, 29.

into the kingdom that Jesus called for, all the while resisting the
temptation of confusing itself with the kingdom.[25]

Caputo argues, on the basis of Jesus' mission and message, for a "theopoetics of the kingdom." "The dangerous memory of the crucified body of Jesus poses a threat to a world organized around the perverted concept of power."[26] The Jesus of the New Testament, although weak and powerless, brought about a reversal whereby "sacred anarchy" invited impossibility, paradox, absurdity, and suffering as the markers of Christian discipleship.[27] This vision of the incursion of the crucified body of Christ demands a response on the part of the church, which understands *itself* to be the broken body of Christ. To imagine Jesus present in our world is to explore those places where Jesus' own message contradicts and challenges the very systems and institutions of power that currently make up the "church." Caputo's vision of a deconstructed Christianity is a philosophical and theological way of driving at the problem of the Constantinization of the church, which was precisely the concern of Kierkegaard's *Attack*. We need not reject the church altogether, or out of hand, to take seriously Caputo's deconstructive vision—for the sake of greater faithfulness in the church and for the sake of deference to the kingdom of God.

For Caputo, the way of postmodern deconstruction is more productive and consistently usable than Kierkegaard's *Attack*. He concludes that, because Kierkegaard was "over the top in those final years . . . it is hard to imagine what any possible institutional church would look like after Kierkegaard."[28] There are two viable responses to Caputo's critique. The first is to point out Kierkegaard's reluctance to approach deconstruction as an external endeavor that focuses on altering circumstances, practices, or institutions in order to bring about renewal. Kierkegaard hesitated to join with or back the causes of sectarian religious renewal movements (such as Anabaptist or free-church Pietist "sects" in Denmark), so long as they advocated a complete breakaway from the institutional state church. For Kierkegaard, this was an unwise solution to a properly diagnosed problem. Simply changing the circumstance or altering the external environment does not fix the problem, if the source of the problem is authentic inwardness (or lack thereof). And yet, as we have seen, Kierkegaard came

25. Ibid., 35.
26. Ibid., 88.
27. Ibid., 86.
28. Ibid., 135–36

to suggest—late in life—that perhaps on rare occasions a formal break is necessary in order to bring about the necessary transformation.

The second response is that one does not need to define in detail (for anyone else) what a Kierkegaardian ecclesiology would look like, for doing so would undercut the necessity of a contextual and particular response. It would mean defining the criterion of authentic community before the process is underway, which would constrain the creativity of the community in living out faith and responding to divine revelation in response to the leading of the Spirit. Maintaining some ambiguity and openness in thinking about what Kierkegaard's ecclesiology would look like is precisely the point. It is also worth noting, incidentally, that the same frustration occurs in appropriating Kierkegaard's insights on hermeneutics and ethics: Where are the specific directions or instructions? For Kierkegaard, just as individual Christians need to remain open to hearing from the Spirit as to how they are to live, so communities require an open space of creativity in responding to God together. Kierkegaard's *kenotic ecclesiology* inspires an instrumental, provisional, "parenthetical" community that upholds Jesus as the prototype against the grain of the world and that follows Jesus courageously and creatively into new territory.

Beyond Christendom: The Emergent Church's Kenotic Ecclesiology

Nicholas Healy writes that "ecclesial cultural identity is constructed as a struggle" to orient itself in the light of its center in Jesus. This struggle for identity takes place through "experimentation, by bricolage, and by retrieval of earlier forms."[29] Churches aware of the precarious and dynamic nature of ecclesial identity attempt to understand their vocation in their own (changing) contexts and circumstances. Furthermore, as Healy notes, the attempt to articulate ecclesial identity through contextual experimentation bears the burden that "conflict, error, and sin are inherent aspects of the concrete church." Therefore, he says, "self-criticism is a necessary element in its further construction."[30]

Doug Pagitt reflects this awareness and confirms the impulse of emergent Christianity to press beyond the confines of Christendom. He says, "It may be quite necessary for some of us to move forward with the way

29. Healy, *Church, World, and the Christian Life*, 175.
30. Ibid.

of Jesus in ways that are not encumbered by the history of Christendom, in the same way the early Christians had to move on with the way of Jesus beyond the temple or synagogue model of Christianity's beginning."[31] He points to the early church's movement beyond the requirements of the law with respect to circumcision as an entry requirement to the community. "It may be," he says, "that in order to be faithful to the gospel that resulted in Christendom, we need not be beholden to Christendom."[32] But if the church acknowledges the possibility and necessity to move beyond elements of Christendom, the question must be raised as to how this can be faithfully and contextually done. Which elements of tradition, he asks, should be left behind, and which should be retained? How does a church separate the wheat from the chaff? The first answer is that it falls to that specific, local community to begin to answer that question, in dialogue with the larger historical traditions and other contemporary communities of faith. Again, specific determinations of the shape and practices of a *kenotic* ecclesiology are difficult to assert, because they can quickly become universal principles.

That said, there are some possible suggestions we can offer as to what shape a *kenotic* ecclesiology, which attempts to move beyond the confines of Christendom, might take today. It makes sense to do that in dialogue with some emergent thinkers regarding the nature of the church. We will limit it to two: (1) church as suspended space, and (2) church as organic, egalitarian ("bottom-up") community. The first suggestion relates to Peter Rollins' image of church as a "suspended space":

> By forming a suspended space in which we participate in the divine kenosis, we allow for the possibility of encountering others beyond the categories that usually define them. We encounter the other beyond the color of his eyes, beyond the contours of her political and religious commitments.[33]

For Rollins, the community of God, when coming together in the fellowship of Christian liturgy, if it is to be authentic, will be a protected environment in which persons are free to genuinely be themselves (to retain their individual "political and religious commitments") but who find their identities transformed in terms of collective participation and engagement with the "other." Emergent churches aim to facilitate communities in which judgment (of the "other") is suspended and in which the divine is

---

31. Pagitt, "Emerging Church and Embodied Theology," 132.
32. Ibid.
33. Rollins, "Worldly Theology of Emerging Christianity," 27.

experienced as mystery. This clearly resonates with Kierkegaard's understanding of the social implications and consequences of authentic subjectivity, as described in *Works of Love*. Christians ought not to interpret and view each other through the lens of external circumstances (power, prestige, beauty, etc.) or even through the grid of personal preference (friendship, erotic love, familial bonds). No single interpretation of the text, whether by a schoolteacher, a plumber, or a pastor, dominates as a reigning interpretation over the community. Furthermore, the "hyphenated" nature of emergent communities suggests that no single strand of the large Christian tradition takes a *de facto* precedence, either. Of course, emergent churches located within specific traditions or denominations will be disproportionately influenced by those traditions. But a sense of openness to diversity and plurality seems to be the norm—and is certainly the ideal. Rollins suggests that this is because "the fundamental Christian event involves exposing the contingency of all interpretations, opening up a desert-like space of negation where *metanoia* can take place (i.e., a substantive change in the individual rather than a mere quantitative improvement)."[34]

The image of church as suspended space helps answer a question raised by Luke Bretherton—one that likely faces many Christians who participate in alternative, renewal forms of church: "So what is to distinguish participation in a local church from having coffee with a friend in Starbucks or a trip to the cinema?" Bretherton's answer is that churches, or rather communities, are "hybrid spaces"; they are connected to their historical past through tradition and are connected to the current "actions of Christ and the Spirit in a particular context and place." The time and place of the event of "church" is "transfigured or translated through orientation of those gathered to the Christian tradition of belief and practice and to the actions of Christ and Spirit in creation."[35] The liturgical idea of suspended space is conceptually linked to the alternative ways in which emergent churches understand their nature as an organization.

The second suggestion, while related to the first, focuses on the organizational structure of the church. Whereas traditional models of church tend to be hierarchical (and often patriarchal in conservative evangelical forms of church life) and relatively static organizationally, emergent Christianity aims at constructing more organic, loosely structured, and egalitarian communities. Often these communities are intentionally smaller

---

34. Ibid.
35. Bretherton, "Beyond the Emerging Church?" 43.

than typical institutional churches, and sometimes without established leadership structures. Emergent Christians believe this more organic style of church life lends itself to more intimacy, to greater sharing of responsibility among its participants (including more opportunity for productive involvement in the community), to greater potential for personal and spiritual development, and to emphasis on the importance of personal and communal authenticity. The downside, perhaps (depending on one's perspective), is that these communities are not necessarily "built to last." As Phyllis Tickle points out, they may spring up for a time, serve a lively, fertile purpose, and then dissipate.[36] They might be more or less spontaneous collectives: bar churches, house churches, or renewal groups within existing congregations. This is not necessarily either good or bad, but it suggests that emergent Christianity has a transient identity. It is not surprising: a movement that "emerged" in part as a critique of institutionalism should not be preoccupied with conserving its own institutional existence.

One way emergent Christians rethink the focus of the church in a more organic, "bottom-up" way is by conceiving of local church communities as "spiritual formation centers." Emergent churches are typically less focused on evangelism and outreach (in contrast, perhaps, with their evangelical "missional church" friends), but they are deeply concerned with discipleship: put in modern terms, they care about spiritual formation and faith development. Kester Brewin, in *Signs of Emergence*, refers to faith development theory, such as that developed by James Fowler in *Stages of Faith: The Psychology of Human Development and the Quest for Meaning*, arguing that most institutionally driven (and hierarchical) churches offer little opportunity for their participants to progress beyond Stage 3 ("Synthetic-Conventional") of spiritual development.[37] At Stage 4, the "Individuative-Reflective" stage, one begins to encounter questions and doubts (anomalies) that need to be addressed with depth and honesty and that must be attended to with empathy on the part of the community. Brewin helpfully summarizes this stage as "the realization that what lies beneath the apparent simplicity of faith is unsymmetrical complexity."[38] Institutional churches are often either not equipped or not predisposed to encourage reflective participants to progress beyond Stage 4 into Stage 5, which Fowler calls "conjunctive faith." A church community that aims

---

36. Tickle, *Emergence Christianity*, 117–19.
37. Brewin, *Signs of Emergence*, 27–34.
38. Ibid., 29.

for the achievement of conjunctive faith understands the importance of spiritual development and personal and relational authenticity. However, as Brewin suggests, the communities best equipped to encourage this as an ideal are those that are more organic, less hierarchical, and less "mechanistic." Participants of institutional churches who are fed up with the structures of the system and who desire to challenge those structures are often squelched by "dictatorial structures" that act "as the curse of death on innovative, creative, and cutting-edge ideas."[39] One author has called these dissidents "reflective exiles."[40] Their questions and critical reflections are no longer welcome within the institution, because they only stir up trouble. Along with the openness to doubt, criticism of Christianity, and theological questions, emergent churches also offer a space for people who are disaffected with traditional church or whose growth has stagnated in traditional church for other reasons. Bretherton believes that emergent Christianity is a more welcoming space for people who are disaffected by "existing or inherited" forms of church. Emerging churches spring up partly as an "attempt to bridge the gap or form church in the church-world hybrid spaces, intersections and networks in which these non-belonging believers move and live and have their being."[41]

Brewin insists that the church, if it is to survive in the days ahead, must "find new peaks out of the valleys by re-emerging as a complex, self-organizing system. . . . [W]e must reestablish ourselves as the *body* of Christ, not the machine of Christ."[42] The focus of a church that would be renewed as a "bottom-up" rather than "top-down" organic community of believers will be driven by a christological understanding that Christ is not an authoritarian dictator, but a suffering servant—a *kenotic* Savior who models the way of voluntary suffering. Brewin recognizes what Kierkegaard understood about Christ's revealing to us a way of suffering rather than a triumphant path of glory and worldly power. Reflection on Christ reveals "God modeling a bottom-up emergent system that can transform us in this new way."[43]

In another section of *What Would Jesus Deconstruct?* Caputo suggests that "an institution modeled *after* deconstruction would be

---

39. Ibid., 84.
40. Harrold, "Deconversion in the Emerging Church," 79–90
41. Bretherton, "Beyond the Emerging Church?" 42.
42. Brewin, *Signs of Emergence*, 85.
43. Ibid., 188.

auto-deconstructive, self-correcting, removed as far as possible from the power games and rigid inflexibility of institutional life . . ."[44] By 1854–55, Kierkegaard had come to believe that the church was too far gone to recognize its own delusions and to realize how far from the New Testament's ideal it had traveled. It could not hear the truth in the corrective voice of a poet, much less could it be "auto-deconstructive" and "self-correcting." The disestablishment Kierkegaard was after, even in his "over the top" attack, is consistent, I believe, with Caputo's call for deconstruction. And yet Kierkegaard would remind any enthusiastic, idealistic reform movement, such as emerging Christianity, that genuine change is always a matter of repentance, prayer, and authentic living more than it is a matter of structural, political, or institutional change. On this point, Caputo has well-placed appreciation for Kierkegaard:

> If the New Testament is a "theory," Kierkegaard said, then it is absurd, and the way not to be scandalized and repelled by the absurdity is what Kierkegaard called "faith," which takes the leap and translates the gospel into existence. Where love is implemented, there is the church. . . . [W]here it is not translated into blood and prayers and tears, into "works of love," no amount of theology, candles, vestments, incense, or polished black hearses can make up the difference (more Kierkegaard).[45]

The emergent movement comprises communities of Christ-followers who desire to recover a sense of authenticity, passion, vulnerability, and intimacy in their lives together. They organize their communities in an intentionally organic way, so that these ideals become (at least conceptually) more attainable than they have seemed to be in institutional forms of church. The caveat here, from a Kierkegaardian point of view, is that when the alteration of the organization becomes the means whereby these aims can be attained, too much freight is given to change in "circumstance" as the hope for renewal, authenticity, and the recovery of the essentially Christian. Nonetheless, it does seem that at some point action must be taken; this is very Kierkegaardian, too. Emergent Christianity's attempt to creatively rethink the nature of the church in this changing world will serve the larger (established) church well—to the extent that it takes notice. Even if the transiency of emergent communities and the lack of institutional structure make propagation a serious challenge, the burst of creativity and

---

44. Caputo, *What Would Jesus Deconstruct?*, 137.
45. Ibid., 124.

critical reflection within emergent Christianity offers—at the very least—an important renewal resource for more empathetic traditional churches. In any case, the question recurs and the refrain continues: How can we attain an existentially authentic faith, both individually and communally? In the context of our ecclesiology discussion, the answer may well lie in a theological deconstruction (and subsequent attempted reconstruction) of institutional forms of church life, which often seem to inhibit authenticity, intimacy, vulnerability, and genuine community. Emergent Christians are working hard to find a better way for this journey. For others, the least they can do is empathize with their quest.

Consistent with the trajectory set forth in *Practice in Christianity*, albeit intensified in his final years, Kierkegaard pointed the way to the disestablishment of the church in favor of the emergence of Christ's kingdom. The church exists in service of the in-breaking of the kingdom of God into temporality. The confrontation with the world occasioned by the action of the historical Christ in his abased life (suffering) and crucifixion opened the way for a new mode of being in the world—one characterized by deep subjectivity and authentic community. This community exists in the eschatological space between the eternal and the temporal, the infinite and the finite, the bound and the free. Kierkegaard's Christology of paradox suggests that the church as an institution—or establishment—must be provisional and temporary, and must give way to the priority of the redemptive presence, or kingdom of God, brought about disruptively in the world through the reign of Christ as the paradoxical one. This means that the church cannot serve itself and ought not understand its mission to be self-preservation. So Jürgen Moltmann says: "It is not the Church that 'has' a mission, but the reverse; Christ's mission creates itself a Church. The mission should not be understood from the perspective of the Church, but the other way round."[46] The church must regularly check its own accumulated habits, its acculturations, commitments, and partnerships with the "powers" and economies of society. It cannot offer itself as an end or become preoccupied with its own self-preservation. Christianity, as an established, institutional, cultural phenomenon, is nonessential. The church defers, bends, and even disappears; like John the Baptist, it must decrease while Christ must increase. When the church becomes its own self-perpetuating institution, when its mission begins to displace the pure, prophetic, and

---

46. Moltmann, *Church in the Power of the Spirit*, 10. Tony Jones has utilized Jürgen Moltmann's theology in developing an emergent ecclesiology in *The Church Is Flat*.

disruptive presence of Christ, it must be disestablished—deconstructed, even—while Christ and his kingdom reappears and reemerges.

There is much in American Christianity to admire and celebrate. And there are countless traditional and institutional communities of God, representing every denomination, who are filled with earnest, grace-filled, mission-inspired people. Furthermore, it would be naïve to suggest that one could extract all institutional elements from a social collective. To "disestablish yourselves" is not necessarily to become a self-identified emergent church or to replace pews with couches and add jazz to liturgy or incense to communion. In other words, as Kierkegaard would no doubt affirm, transforming the aesthetics is not yet to transform the religious—aesthetics alone has little to do with authenticity, inwardness, and subjectivity. In a journal entry, Kierkegaard makes this clear: "Let us not then—in order to divert!—convene synods or—in order to gain postponement!—appoint commissions. No, if something like this [reform] is to be done, then let a universal day of repentance and prayer be prescribed."[47] Structural revolutions attempt but do not necessarily address—and they certainly do not solve—the question of one's inward relation to God. In fact, they often only put off true repentance. Attempts at structural and institutional reform are too easily sidetracked and encumbered by mediocrity of the human spirit. Furthermore, revolutions have a way of substituting one idol and one ideology for another. Kierkegaard believed that the most important issue was authenticity: inwardness—the development of the person as a self before God. For reformist-minded and renewal-minded Christians, this is a good reminder. But it would be naïve to suggest that there is no connection between inwardness and externality, or internal dispositions and outward structures. Thus, movements such as emergent Christianity have a constructive role to play in challenging existing structures, deconstructing persistent idols/ideologies, and exploring new, creative ways to live into the authenticity and passion of New Testament faith. In any case, the primary issue is not the "externals"—the material or organizational structures—

---

47. *Pap.* XI3 B 32. Kester Brewin offers a similar warning in his reflections on the emerging church: "I want to argue that in the Emergent Church the emphasis will be on being the train, rather than trainspotting: rather than trying to import culture into church and make it 'cool,' we need instead to become 'wombs of the divine' and completely rebirth the church into a host culture. So while the excitement over the emerging church is to be welcomed, I think we need to advance with caution for fear of these things precipitating a revolution that will not last, and bringing changes that will be just tactical." *Signs of Emergence*, 92–93.

Against Christendom

but the passion through which persons pursue the God-relationship and the devotion with which they perform works of love in the world. This, of course, is not unrelated to a deep, theological understanding of what it means to be Christian and what it means to be the "people of God."

Conclusion

If Butler Bass (with the statistics she cites) is right, Christianity is in the midst of a shift. Kierkegaard offers us great insight into navigating this difficult terrain by advocating a cruciform, Christ-centered, epistemologically humble, and holistic (faith organically tied to action) understanding of Christianity's purpose in the world. Kierkegaard's disestablishment of Christianity was a reestablishment of a gospel Christology of paradox, suffering, and the cross. In Kierkegaard, one finds the seeds for a deep, passionate logic of a radically decentered, self-deconstructing, New Testament ecclesiology—an ecclesiology driven more by authenticity, inward transformation, and self-sacrifice than by a particular polity, tradition, denomination, or creed. In the end, neither Kierkegaard nor emergent Christianity is the cure for Christendom; Christ and the Spirit of God are. But for those who wish to rethink church in our contemporary, complex, and (still) postmodern society, who want to shake loose the chains of the establishment, and who long to discover a fresh, authentic passion in relation to the eternal God in Christ, Kierkegaard will prove a provocative and inspiring—if, at times, perplexing—dialogue partner. But be warned: it is dangerous to take a prophet for a partner.

CONCLUSION
Reclaiming the Restlessness of Faith

"In Christendom he also is a Christian, goes to church every Sunday, listens to and understands the pastor, indeed, they have a mutual understanding; he dies, the pastor ushers him into eternity for ten rix-dollars—but a self he was not, and a self he did not become."[1]

"No, my friend, faith is a restless thing."[2]

KIERKEGAARD, AS "EMERGING PROPHET," compels us to think about what Christianity, the church, and a new apologetic might look like in this early part of the twenty-first century. This is in many respects a chaotic time, a confusing time, and, like all "times," transitional. He compels us to think a little harder about the authenticity of faith and about the authenticity of our Christian witness in the world. In response to Kierkegaard's prophetic voice, we ought to give some careful reflection regarding how we might pursue a deeper authenticity and greater motivation for performing works of love. Emergent Christianity is already on the move in search of a deeper authenticity and is already articulating a creative vision for the church in an age beyond the trappings of static forms of institutional religion. As we

1. *SUD*, 52.
2. *FSE*, 18.

circle back to an early discussion in this book, we should notice that this quest for authenticity—individually and communally—begins with serious attention to the nature of the self as a dynamically evolving, integrated, and intricately relational being.

For Kierkegaard, the notion of "self" lies at the heart of the question, who am I? Recent movements in psychology have shown that the self is constructed not by the individual in a vacuum—a Cartesian, rationalist skeptic, for example—but largely through relationship with others. What do my parents think of me? My friends? How do *you* perceive me? We all take such things into account, at least partially, as we perceive ourselves. As Stephen Evans puts it, "Self-knowledge has a social dimension."[3]

In a discourse titled "To Gain One's Soul in Patience," Kierkegaard offers an exhortation to relinquish control of the finite in order to "gain" the eternal. A person is a synthesis of the temporal and eternal, of freedom and necessity, with the potential to become an authentic self, properly related to God. In Kierkegaard's words: every person is confronted with the capacity to "gain one's soul."[4] As such, every human being is a struggle; every person is the focal point of striving in relation to eternity's rewards. But this struggle for eternity, for inwardness and personal authenticity is deeply connected to the temporal, the tangible, and the actual; the vertical dimension of salvation involves the horizontal, or the social.

Along with a social dimension, self-knowledge has a *theological* dimension. Becoming a self and acquiring existential meaning requires that one become, as we have seen, a theological self—a person whose identity, outlook, and actions are constituted by one's ontological relation to God, by one's relation to others, and by one's relation to oneself (we might say: coming to terms with who one is—or, in a sense, *ought* to be). The development of selfhood is, then, a constantly shifting task. In Kierkegaard's schemata, the authentic self is the one in whom the relation between the self and God (eternity) has become primarily constitutive of the self. The polarities that constitute the divided self have merged, in a sense, resulting in a synthesis in which something greater and deeper gives meaning to one's life.

In authentic selfhood, one cannot cleanly separate between one's constitutive, dialectically constituted "parts." The criterion of the authenticity of self is a synthesis of freedom and spontaneity, responsibility and down-to-earth seriousness, courage and action. The authentic self acknowledges

---

3. Evans, "The Relational Self: Psychological and Theological Perspectives," 78.
4. See the discourse, "To Gain One's Soul in Patience," in *EUD*, 159–76.

the way things are, while recognizing they are not what they could—or should—be. The authentic self embraces community, while accepting the centrality of the task of subjective development "before God." The authentic self accepts the finitude of human existence (its suffering, brokenness, and strange paradoxes) without despairing. The authentic self respects the mystery of the transcendent and the beauty of the poetic, and refuses to dance darkly down the path of narcissism and nihilism. The authentic self refuses to be given over to the sickness unto death. The authentic self chooses herself by recognizing eternity's claim upon her and opening herself to the reality of God and the embrace of the other.

The church, the people of God, ought to be communities in which persons learn how to become selves, in intimate relation to each other. They learn together that to be human is to be open to God, constituted by their relationship to the God of the gospel. They collectively commit to follow the way of Jesus in the power of the Spirit. The church ought to be a training center for works of love.[5] The people of God should reflect in their forms of life and interactivity that "something more," inviting the deeper places of the self to voice its passions, articulate its doubts, and search out its desires, overriding that inauthentic self, that *imposter*—what St. Paul called "the old man." Become a new creation! The new has come.

As modern persons, Kierkegaard suggests, we are too often unaware of the crucial distinction between faith and knowledge, and we too often assume that acquisition of knowledge or understanding of and adherence to doctrine brings us everything we need in terms of the religious—now it is just a matter of sanctification, of putting that knowledge into practice. But Kierkegaard tells us that it simply does not work this way, so long as knowledge is understood as cognitive, objective knowledge rather than subjective, existential, and relational knowledge. The New Testament invites us to be doers of the Word, not hearers only:

> Any mere hearing of the Word is infinitely more imperfect than the doing, not only because the doing is superior but because in comparison with the exactitude of the doing any oral communication is very imperfect, both in its brevity and in its prolixity. Therefore knowledge of one's own soul, if one wants to regard it as a gaining, is a self-deception, because even in its greatest completeness it still

---

5. See McLaren, *New Kind of Christianity*, 170.

is but a hint of what manifests itself in its definiteness during the gaining.[6]

True, existential, subjective knowledge is acquired through action—through obedience—not solely or even primarily through academic, doctrinal, theological, or even biblical knowledge. Kierkegaard says that the world deludes a person into thinking that he possesses true knowledge; but in truth, this knowledge possesses her.[7] Kierkegaard wants us to think about selfhood as an existential task in which the goal is to be transformed as a person—but that takes a lifetime. A person becomes a self, and gains "one's soul in patience." It is a process that takes a lifetime of striving, struggle, failure, and doubt. One navigates this struggle through passion, patience, prayer, repentance, and action.

FROM PASSION TO ACTION

As we have seen throughout this book, for Kierkegaard, the essentially Christian is marked by a willingness to break the cycle of an objective, dispassionate approach to life and Christianity, through the personal appropriation of subjective truth. This appropriation means that a shift has taken place: from objectivity to subjectivity and from passivity to action. The authentic inwardness of one's passion will result in the outward manifestation of action, of "collisions" with the world. Passion giving rise to action is evidence of having rightly understood divine revelation and of having an adequate grasp on concrete reality—one's situation. From the perspective of the essentially Christian, only through action can true understanding actually be acquired.

In *Judge for Yourself!*, Kierkegaard's reflection on the Pentecostal experience of the early church, he says that "sobriety," Christianly understood, is "to come so close to oneself in one's understanding, in one's knowing, that all one's understanding becomes action."[8] Kierkegaard claims that modern cultured people have reversed the order. They have sought to understand conceptually, theoretically, and abstractly without having that truth impact their selves holistically and from the beginning of the knowing process. Essential truth can only be acquired by *doing* it, by *living* in it, and by *act-*

6. *EUD*, 173.
7. *EUD*, 172–73.
8. *JFY*, 115.

ing in accordance with it in one's life. Christianity teaches, according to Kierkegaard, that the only person who is completely sober is the person whose understanding is action:

> And so it ought to be. Your understanding must immediately be action. Immediately! Alas, but this is not the way it is with us human beings! When we have understood something, it takes ages before there is action or before the reproduction is an action. In the right relation, however, action follows immediately, and then, just because of this, the reproduction is your understanding, accurate, complete, and unabridged.[9]

This prophetic message is no more or less relevant for emergent Christianity than it is for any other stream or tradition of the church. It is no more—or less—relevant for you than it is for me. Nonetheless, the emergent leaders and theologians I have discussed in this book show that the emerging church is uniquely prepared and willing to receive this message.

Emergent Christians reveal a willingness to push past the established patterns, procedures, and theories (or theologies) that Christianity has inherited in the modern world. When understanding means action—and when understanding derives from action—action must be recognized as primary. What matters is following Christ in obedience, even if that brings suffering and "collisions" with the world. What is most important is getting on the move, getting to the task of becoming selves and communities of selves who perform works of love for others. But doing this may require rethinking—and deconstructing—inherited, embedded institutions, frameworks, and systems that, while barely noticeable, are profoundly influential.

Every person is a site of a potentially passionate struggle, with grave consequences hanging in the balance. Every community of persons—every church—is a collective site of religious and existential struggle. We are confronted with the great challenges of life, death, meaning, and truth. Will we shrink back from the struggle—and be satisfied with less than our potential? We will be content with the status quo? Will we be happy with church buildings, "successful" programs, and budget increases? Or will we penetrate deeper into the mystery of the "self" and think about what that means not just for us as individuals, but also for those collectives of selves called the church?

Kierkegaard's view of the essentially Christian and his emphasis on the authenticity of the self can be fertile soil for the cultivation of an emergent

---

9. *JFY*, 120.

Christian theology. An emergent theology and practice that affirms its own impulses toward constructing a new kind of Christianity—this is not actually *new*, but as old as the New Testament itself. A new kind of Christianity based on the radicalism of divine forgiveness, embracing the way of suffering, centered on the absolute paradox, and motivated to do works of love.

A CONCLUDING, RESTLESS THOUGHT

Faith is restless because it is, objectively speaking, risky. Christians ought not to rest content with the commodities of objectivity—bought and sold in modernity—in either its liberal or fundamentalist forms. The solution is not to hitch our wagons to any other "ism" or ideology, including postmodernity; nonetheless, it seems that the postmodern turn creates some intellectual (epistemological, hermeneutical) breathing room, and a cultural pause, for a conscious attempt at deepening the authenticity of Christian faith and reconsidering the meaning of "church." In doing so, a few key themes regarding the "restlessness of faith" deserve final reflection. First, recall that because faith is its own ground, doubt is always the other side of faith, and the answer to doubt is not rational argument but passion and action impelled by a deeper, experiential (but still theological) vision. This faith is accompanied by the passion of conviction rather than by the security of certainty. Second, the restlessness of faith undercuts our tendencies toward idolatrous self-congratulation, superiority, and—here in the United States—the disastrous attempt at a synthesis of religious and national identity. Given its historical tendencies toward triumphalism, and even violent behavior toward others, the church cannot trust in its own, self-congratulatory ability to mediate the presence of God to the world. It must, in faith, rely on the transformational power of God to work through its humble brokenness as it opens itself to both God and others. Third, the restlessness of faith restores personal wholeness to the self who undertakes a disposition of humility toward and dependence on God. This transformative approach is something that constantly must be won; that is, it must be fought for and sought after by both individuals and communities who value and strive for authenticity. The people of God, ought not to glory in past "achievements" and "victories" (the "church triumphant") but should continually be renewing their faith, reforming their practice, and humbling themselves in the attempt to follow Jesus on the narrow way of suffering. The postmodern people of God should continue to hear the prophetic call of Kierkegaard—that the way of Christianity provides a continual challenge and purpose to live simply, with a purity of heart, sharing a common vision to testify to the absolute paradox and to the paradoxical kingdom of God. May we all, emergent Christian or not, embrace the restlessness of faith and see where that takes us.

BIBLIOGRAPHY

Adam, A. K. M. "Integral and Differential Hermeneutics." In *Faithful Interpretation: Reading the Bible in a Postmodern World*, 81–104. Minneapolis: Fortress, 2006.
Anderson, Ray Sherman. *An Emergent Theology for Emerging Churches*. Downers Grove, IL: InterVarsity, 2006.
———. *The Shape of Practical Theology: Empowering Ministry with Theological Praxis*. Downers Grove, IL: InterVarsity, 2001.
Barnett, Christopher B. *Kierkegaard, Pietism and Holiness*. Burlington, VT: Ashgate, 2010.
Barrett, Lee C. *Kierkegaard*. Nashville: Abingdon, 2010.
Bass, Diana Butler. *Christianity After Religion: The End of Church and the Birth of a New Spiritual Awakening*. New York: HarperOne, 2012.
Bauckham, Richard. *Bible and Mission: Christian Witness in a Postmodern World*. Grand Rapids: Baker, 2003.
Beck, Richard Allan. *The Authenticity of Faith: The Varieties and Illusions of Religious Experience*. Abilene, TX: Abilene Christian University Press, 2012.
Beilby, James K. "Contemporary Religious Epistemology: Some Key Aspects for the Scripture Project." In *The Scripture Project: The Bible and Biblical Authority in the New Millennium*, edited by D. A. Carson. Grand Rapids: Eerdmans, forthcoming.
Bellah, Robert N. "Biblical Religion and Social Science in the Modern World." *NICM Journal for Jews and Christians in Higher Education* 6 (1982) 8–22.
Bellah, Robert N., et al. *Habits of the Heart: Individualism and Commitment in American Life*. Berkeley: University of California Press, 1985.
Benson, Bruce Ellis. *Graven Ideologies: Nietzsche, Derrida & Marion on Modern Idolatry*. Downers Grove, IL: InterVarsity, 2002.
Best, Steven, and Douglas Kellner. *The Postmodern Turn*. New York: Guilford, 1997.
Billings, J. Todd. *The Word of God for the People of God: An Entryway to the Theological Interpretation of Scripture*. Grand Rapids: Eerdmans, 2010.
Bird, Warren. "Emerging Church Movement." In *Encyclopedia of Religion in America*, edited by C. H. Lippy and P. W. Williams. Washington, DC: CQ, 2010.
Blount, Douglas K. "A New Kind of Interpretation." In *Evangelicals Engaging Emergent: A Discussion of the Emergent Church Movement*. Edited by William David Henard and Adam W. Greenway, 109–28. Nashville: B. & H. Academic, 2009.
Blue, Debbie. *From Stone to Living Word: Letting the Bible Live Again*. Grand Rapids: Brazos, 2008.

Bibliography

Bonhoeffer, Dietrich. *Letters and Papers from Prison*. Edited by John W. de Gruchy. Translated by Isabel Best. Dietrich Bonhoeffer Works 8. Minneapolis: Fortress, 2010.

Bretherton, Luke. "Beyond the Emerging Church?" In *Remembering Our Future: Explorations in Deep Church*, edited by Andrew Walker and Luke Bretherton, 30–58. Milton Keynes, UK: Paternoster, 2007.

Brewin, Kester. *Signs of Emergence: A Vision for Church that Is Organic/Networked/Decentralized/Bottom-Up/Communal/Flexible/Always Evolving*. Grand Rapids: Baker, 2007.

Brueggemann, Walter. *The Book that Breathes New Life: Scriptural Authority and Biblical Theology*. Minneapolis: Fortress, 2004.

———. *The Prophetic Imagination*. Philadelphia: Fortress, 1978.

———. *Texts Under Negotiation: The Bible and Postmodern Imagination*. Minneapolis: Fortress, 1993.

Caputo, John D. *How to Read Kierkegaard*. London: Granta, 2007.

———. *Radical Hermeneutics: Repetition, Deconstruction, and the Hermeneutic Project*. Bloomington: Indiana University Press, 1987.

———. *What Would Jesus Deconstruct? The Good News of Postmodernism for the Church*. Grand Rapids: Baker, 2007.

Carson, D. A. *Becoming Conversant with the Emerging Church: Understanding a Movement and Its Implications*. Grand Rapids: Zondervan, 2005.

Collins, James Daniel. *The Mind of Kierkegaard*. Chicago: Regnery, 1953.

Conder, Tim, and Daniel Rhodes. *Free for All: Rediscovering the Bible in Community*. Grand Rapids: Baker, 2009.

Corcoran, Kevin. "Who's Afraid of Philosophical Realism?" In *Church in the Present Tense: A Candid Look at What's Emerging*, edited by Scot McKnight et al., 3–22. Grand Rapids: Brazos, 2011.

Crisp, Oliver D., and Michael C. Rea, editors. *Analytic Theology: New Essays in the Philosophy of Theology*. Oxford: Oxford University Press, 2009.

Davenport, John J., Anthony Rudd, Alasdair C. MacIntyre, and Philip L. Quinn. *Kierkegaard After MacIntyre: Essays on Freedom, Narrative, and Virtue*. Chicago: Open Court, 2001.

Deuser, Hermann. "Religious Dialectics and Christology." In *The Cambridge Companion to Kierkegaard*, edited by Alastair Hannay and Gordon Daniel Marino, 376–96. Cambridge: Cambridge University Press, 1998.

DeYoung, Kevin, and Ted Kluck. *Why We're Not Emergent: By Two Guys Who Should Be*. Chicago: Moody, 2008.

Dooley, Mark. *The Politics of Exodus: Søren Kierkegaard's Ethics of Responsibility*. New York: Fordham University Press, 2001.

Dupré, Louis. *Kierkegaard as Theologian: The Dialectic of Christian Existence*. New York: Sheed & Ward, 1963.

Elrod, John W. *Kierkegaard and Christendom*. Princeton: Princeton University Press, 1981.

Emmanuel, Steven M. *Kierkegaard and the Concept of Revelation*. Albany: State University of New York Press, 1996.

Evans, C. Stephen. "Externalist Epistemology, Subjectivity, and Christian Knowledge: Plantinga and Kierkegaard." In *Kierkegaard on Faith and the Self: Collected Essays*, 183–208. Waco: Baylor University Press, 2006.

———. *Kierkegaard: An Introduction*. Cambridge: Cambridge University Press, 2009.

———. "Kierkegaard and Plantinga on Belief in God: Subjectivity as the Ground of Properly Basic Beliefs." In *Kierkegaard on Faith and the Self: Collected Essays*, 169–82. Waco: Baylor University Press, 2006.

———. "Kierkegaard on Religious Authority: The Problem of the Criterion." *Faith and Philosophy* 17 (2000) 48–67.

———. *Kierkegaard's "Fragments" and "Postscript": The Religious Philosophy of Johannes Climacus*. Atlantic Highlands, NJ: Humanities, 1983.

———. "The Relational Self: Psychological and Theological Perspectives." In *Judeo-Christian Perspectives on Psychology: Human Nature, Motivation, and Change*, edited by W. R. Miller and H. D. Delaney, 73–93. Washington, DC: American Psychological Association, 2005.

———. *Søren Kierkegaard's Christian Psychology: Insight for Counseling & Pastoral Care*. Grand Rapids: Ministry Resources Library, 1990.

Ferguson, Harvie. *Modernity and Subjectivity: Body, Soul, Spirit*. Charlottesville: University Press of Virginia, 2000.

Ferreira, M. Jamie. *Kierkegaard*. Malden, MA: Wiley-Blackwell, 2009.

Fishburn, Janet Forsythe. "Soren Kierkegaard, Exegete." *Interpretation* 39 (1985) 229–45.

Gadamer, Hans-Georg. *Truth and Method*. Translated by Joel Weinsheimer and Donald G. Marshall. 2nd ed. New York: Crossroad, 1989.

Garff, Joakim. *Søren Kierkegaard: A Biography*. Princeton: Princeton University Press, 2005.

Gibbs, Eddie, and Ryan K. Bolger. *Emerging Churches: Creating Christian Community in Postmodern Cultures*. Grand Rapids: Baker, 2005.

Green, Garrett. *Theology, Hermeneutics, and Imagination: The Crisis of Interpretation at the End of Modernity*. Cambridge: Cambridge University Press, 2000.

Grenz, Stanley. "Articulating the Christian Belief-Mosaic: Theological Method after the Demise of Foundationalism." In *Evangelical Futures: A Conversation on Theological Method*, edited by John G. Stackhouse, Jr., 107–36. Vancouver: Regent College, 2000.

Grenz, Stanley J., and John R. Franke. *Beyond Foundationalism: Shaping Theology in a Postmodern Context*. Louisville: Westminster John Knox, 2001.

Groothuis, Douglas R. *Truth Decay: Defending Christianity against the Challenges of Postmodernism*. Downers Grove, IL: InterVarsity, 2000.

Guder, Darrell L., editor. *Missional Church: A Vision for the Sending of the Church in North America*. Grand Rapids: Eerdmans, 1998.

Hall, Amy Laurel. "Polk's Biblical Kierkegaard." In *Søren Kierkegaard Newsletter* 36 (1998) 4–5. Online: http://www.stolaf.edu/collections/kierkegaard/newsletters/Newsletter36.pdf.

Hall, Douglas John. "Metamorphosis: From Christendom to Diaspora." In *Confident Witness—Changing World: Rediscovering the Gospel in North America*, edited by Craig Van Gelder, 67–89. Grand Rapids: Eerdmans, 1999.

Harrold, Philip. "Deconversion in the Emergent Church." *International Journal for the Study of the Christian Church* 6.1 (2006) 79–90.

Hauerwas, Stanley. *Unleashing the Scripture: Freeing the Bible from Captivity to America*. Nashville: Abingdon, 1993.

Hays, Richard B. "Ecclesiology and Ethics in 1 Corinthians." *Ex Auditu* 10 (1994) 31–43.

Healy, Nicholas M. *Church, World, and the Christian Life: Practical-Prophetic Ecclesiology*. Cambridge: Cambridge University Press, 2000.

Bibliography

Henard, William David, and Adam W. Greenway. *Evangelicals Engaging Emergent: A Discussion of the Emergent Church Movement.* Nashville: B. & H. Academic, 2009.

Henriksen, Jan-Olav. *The Reconstruction of Religion: Lessing, Kierkegaard, and Niezsche.* Grand Rapids: Eerdmans, 2001.

Heywood Thomas, John. *The Legacy of Kierkegaard.* Eugene, OR: Cascade Books, 2011.

Jones, Tony. *The Church Is Flat: The Relational Ecclesiology of the Emerging Church Movement.* Minneapolis: JoPa Group, 2011.

———. *The New Christians: Dispatches from the Emergent Frontier.* San Francisco: Jossey-Bass, 2008.

Keel, Tim. "Leading from the Margins: The Role of Imagination in Our Changing Context." In *An Emergent Manifesto of Hope,* edited by Doug Pagitt and Tony Jones, 225-34. Grand Rapids: Baker, 2007.

Kierkegaard, Søren. *Christian Discourses; The Crisis and a Crisis in the Life of an Actress.* Edited and translated by Howard V. Hong and Edna H. Hong. Princeton: Princeton University Press, 1997.

———. *The Concept of Anxiety: A Simple Psychologically Orienting Deliberation on the Dogmatic Issue of Hereditary Sin.* Translated by Howard V. Hong and Reidar Thomte. Princeton: Princeton University Press, 1980.

———. *Concluding Unscientific Postscript to Philosophical Fragments.* Translated by Howard V. Hong and Edna H. Hong. Princeton: Princeton University Press, 1992.

———. *Eighteen Upbuilding Discourses.* Translated by Howard V. Hong and Edna H. Hong. Princeton: Princeton University Press, 1990.

———. *Either/Or Part I.* Translated by Howard V. Hong and Edna H. Hong. Princeton: Princeton University Press, 1987.

———. *Fear and Trembling.* Edited and translated by Howard V. Hong and Edna H. Hong. Princeton: Princeton University Press, 1983.

———. *For Self-Examination; Judge for Yourself!* Translated by Howard V. Hong and Edna H. Hong. Princeton: Princeton University Press, 1990.

———. *Kierkegaard's Attack Upon "Christendom," 1854-1855.* Translated by Walter Lowrie. Princeton: Princeton University Press, 1968.

———. *The Moment and Late Writings.* Translated by Howard V. Hong and Edna H. Hong. Princeton: Princeton University Press, 2009.

———. *Philosophical Fragments, Johannes Climacus.* Translated by Howard V. Hong and Edna H. Hong. Princeton: Princeton University Press, 1985.

———. *The Point of View.* Translated by Howard V. Hong and Edna H. Hong. Princeton: Princeton University Press, 2009.

———. *Practice in Christianity.* Translated by Howard V. Hong and Edna H. Hong. Princeton: Princeton University Press, 1991.

———. *The Sickness Unto Death: A Christian Psychological Exposition for Upbuilding and Awakening.* Translated by Howard V. Hong and Edna H. Hong. Princeton: Princeton University Press, 1980.

———. *Søren Kierkegaard's Journals and Papers.* Translated by Howard V. Hong, Edna H. Hong, and Gregor Malantschuk. Princeton: Princeton University Press, 1967.

———. *Søren Kierkegaard's Papirer.* Edited by P. A. Heiberg, V. Kuhr, and E. Torsting. 16 vols. In 25 vols., 2nd ed., edited by N. Thulstrup, with an index by N. J. Cappelørn. Copenhagen: Gyldendal, 1968-78.

———. *Stages on Life's Way.* Translated by Walter Lowrie. New York: Schocken, 1967.

———. *Three Discourses on Imagined Occasions*. Translated by Howard V. Hong and Edna H. Hong. Princeton: Princeton University Press, 2009.

———. *Upbuilding Discourses in Various Spirits*. Translated by Howard V. Hong and Edna H. Hong. Princeton: Princeton University Press, 1993.

———. *Without Authority*. Translated by Howard V. Hong and Edna H. Hong. Princeton: Princeton University Press, 1997.

———. *Works of Love*. Translated by Howard V. Hong and Edna H. Hong. Princeton: Princeton University Press, 1995.

Kraus, C. Norman. *The Authentic Witness: Credibility and Authority*. Grand Rapids: Eerdmans, 1979.

Laughery, Gregory J. "Evangelicalism and Philosophy." In *Futures of Evangelicalism*, edited by Craig G. Bartholomew, Robin A. Parry, and Andrew West, 259–60. Grand Rapids: Kregel, 2004.

Law, David R. "Cheap Grace and the Cost of Discipleship in Kierkegaard's *For Self-Examination*." In *For Self-Examination and Judge for Yourself!*, edited by Robert L. Perkins, 111–42. International Kierkegaard Commentary 21. Macon, GA: Mercer University Press, 2002.

———. *Kierkegaard as Negative Theologian*. Oxford: Clarendon, 1993.

———. "Kierkegaard on Truth." *Downside Review* 116 (1998) 103–7.

———. "Kierkegaard's Anti-Ecclesiology: The Attack on 'Christendom,' 1854–55." *International Journal for the Study of the Christian Church* 7 (2007) 86–108.

Lowrie, Walter. *A Short Life of Kierkegaard*. Princeton: Princeton University Press, 1942.

Lynch, Gordon. *The New Spirituality: An Introduction to Progressive Belief in the Twenty-First Century*. London: Tauris, 2007.

Lyotard, Jean-François. *The Postmodern Condition: A Report on Knowledge*. Minneapolis: University of Minnesota Press, 1984.

MacKinnon, Donald M. *The Stripping of the Altars: The Gore Memorial Lecture Delivered on 5 November 1968 in Westminster Abbey and Other Papers and Essays on Related Topics*. London: Collins; Fontana, 1969.

Mahn, Jason A. *Fortunate Fallibility: Kierkegaard and the Power of Sin*. New York: Oxford University Press, 2011.

Martensen, H. L. *Berlingske Tidende* No. 302, December 28, 1854.

Mathewes, Charles T. *The Republic of Grace: Augustinian Thoughts for Dark Times*. Grand Rapids: Eerdmans, 2010.

McGowan, A. T. B. *The Divine Spiration of Scripture: Challenging Evangelical Perspectives*. Nottingham, UK: Apollos, 2007.

McKnight, Scot. "Atonement and Gospel." In *Church in the Present Tense: A Candid Look at What's Emerging*, edited by Scot McKnight et al., 123–40. Grand Rapids: Brazos, 2011.

———. *The Blue Parakeet: Rethinking How You Read the Bible*. Grand Rapids: Zondervan, 2008.

McLaren, Brian D. *A Generous Orthodoxy: Why I Am a Missional, Evangelical, Post/Protestant, Liberal/Conservative, Mystical/Poetic, Biblical, Charismatic/Contemplative, Fundamentalist/Calvinist, Anabaptist/Anglican, Methodist, Catholic, Green, Incarnational, Depressed-yet-Hopeful, Emergent, Unfinished Christian*. El Cajon, CA: Emergent YS, 2004.

———. *A New Kind of Christianity: Ten Questions that Are Transforming the Faith*. New York: HarperOne, 2011.

Bibliography

McLaren, Brian D., and Anthony Campolo. *Adventures in Missing the Point: How the Culture-Controlled Church Neutered the Gospel.* El Cajon, CA: Emergent YS, 2003.

Meek, Esther L. *Longing to Know.* Grand Rapids: Brazos, 2003.

———. *Loving to Know: Introducing Covenant Epistemology.* Eugene, OR: Cascade Books, 2011.

Minear, Paul S., and Paul S. Morimoto. *Kierkegaard and the Bible: An Index.* Princeton: Princeton Theological Seminary, 1953.

Moltmann, Jürgen. *The Church in the Power of the Spirit: A Contribution to Messianic Ecclesiology.* Translated by Margaret Kohl. New York: Harper & Row, 1977.

Moody, Katharine Sarah. "I Hate Your Church: What I Want Is My Kingdom: Emerging Spiritualties in the UK Emerging Church Milieu." *The Expository Times* 121.10 (2010) 495–503.

Pagitt, Doug. *A Christianity Worth Believing: Hope-Filled, Open-Armed, Alive-and-Well Faith for the Left Out, Left Behind, and Let Down in Us All.* San Francisco: Jossey-Bass, 2008.

———. "The Emerging Church and Embodied Theology." In *Listening to the Beliefs of Emerging Churches: Five Perspectives,* edited by Robert Webber, 119–43. Grand Rapids: Zondervan, 2007.

Penner, Myron B, editor. *Christianity and the Postmodern Turn: Six Views.* Grand Rapids: Brazos, 2005.

Polanyi, Michael. *Personal Knowledge: Towards a Post-Critical Philosophy.* New York: Harper & Row, 1964.

Polk, Timothy. *The Biblical Kierkegaard: Reading by the Rule of Faith.* Macon, GA: Mercer University Press, 1997.

Pons, Jolita. *Stealing a Gift: Kierkegaard's Pseudonyms and the Bible.* New York: Fordham University Press, 2004.

Rae, Murray. *Kierkegaard and Theology.* London: T. & T. Clark, 2010.

Rea, Michael C., and Oliver D. Crisp, editors. *Analytic Theology: New Essays in the Philosophy of Theology.* Oxford: Oxford University Press, 2009.

Roberts, Kyle A. "Francis Schaeffer: How Not to Read Kierkegaard." In *Kierkegaard's Influence on Theology, Tome II: Anglophone and Scandinavian Protestant Theology,* edited by Jon Stewart, 173–90. Farnham, UK: Ashgate, 2012.

———. "Lazarus: Kierkegaard's Use of a Destitute Beggar and a Resurrected Friend." In *Kierkegaard and the Bible,* edited by Lee C. Barrett and Jon Stewart, 139–50. Farnham, UK: Ashgate, 2010.

———. "The Living Word and the Word of God: The Pietist Impulse in Kierkegaard and Grundtvig." In *The Pietist Impulse in Christianity,* edited by Christian T. Collins Winn et al., 120–34. Eugene, OR: Pickwick Publications, 2011.

Rollins, Peter. "Biting the Hand that Feeds: An Apology for Encouraging Tension between the Established Church and Emerging Churches." In *Evaluating Fresh Expressions,* edited by Louise Nelstrop and Martyn Percy, 71–84. Norwich, UK: Canterbury, 2008.

———. *The Fidelity of Betrayal: Towards a Church beyond Belief.* Brewster, MA: Paraclete, 2008.

———. *How (Not) to Speak of God.* Brewster, MA: Paraclete, 2006.

———. "Transformance Art: Reconfiguring the Social Self." In *Church in the Present Tense: A Candid Look at What's Emerging,* edited by Scot McKnight et al., 89–104. Grand Rapids: Brazos, 2011.

———. "The Worldly Theology of Emerging Christianity." In *Church in the Present Tense: A Candid Look at What's Emerging*, edited by Scot McKnight et al., 23–38. Grand Rapids: Brazos, 2011.

Rubenstein, Richard L. *The Age of Triage: Fear and Hope in an Overcrowded World*. Boston: Beacon, 1983.

Schrag, Calvin O. "The Kierkegaard-Effect in the Shaping of the Contours of Modernity." In *Kierkegaard in Post/Modernity*, edited by Martin Joseph Matuštík and Merold Westphal, 1–17. Bloomington: Indiana University Press, 1995.

Simpson, Christopher Ben. *The Truth Is the Way: Kierkegaard's Theologia Viatorum*. Eugene, OR: Cascade Books, 2011.

Sparks, Kenton L. *God's Word in Human Words: An Evangelical Appropriation of Critical Biblical Scholarship*. Grand Rapids: Baker, 2008.

Sponheim, Paul R. *Kierkegaard on Christ and Christian Coherence*. New York: Harper & Row, 1968.

Taylor, Charles. *A Secular Age*. Cambridge: Belknap Press of Harvard University Press, 2007.

Thiselton, Antony C. "'Behind' and 'In Front Of' the Text: Language, Reference and Indeterminacy." In *After Pentecost: Language and Biblical Interpretation*, edited by Craig G. Bartholomew et al., 97–130. Carlisle, UK: Paternoster, 2001.

Tickle, Phyllis. *Emergence Christianity: What It Is, Where It Is Going, and Why It Matters*. Grand Rapids: Baker, 2012.

———. *The Great Emercence: How Christianity Is Changing and Why*. Grand Rapids: Baker, 2008.

Treier, Daniel J. *Introducing Theological Interpretation of Scripture: Recovering a Christian Practice*. Grand Rapids: Baker, 2008.

Vanhoozer, Kevin J. *Is There a Meaning in This Text? The Bible, the Reader, and the Morality of Literary Knowledge*. Grand Rapids: Zondervan, 1998.

Van Huyssteen, J. Wentzel. *Essays in Postfoundationalist Theology*. Grand Rapids: Eerdmans, 1997.

———. *The Shaping of Rationality: Toward Interdisciplinarity in Theology and Science*. Grand Rapids: Eerdmans, 1999.

Walsh, Sylvia. *Kierkegaard: Thinking Christianly in an Existential Mode*. Oxford: Oxford University Press, 2009.

———. *Living Christianly: Kierkegaard's Dialectic of Christian Existence*. University Park: Pennsylvania State University Press, 2005.

Ward, Karen. "The Emerging Church and Communal Theology." In *Listening to the Beliefs of Emerging Churches: Five Perspectives*, edited by Robert Webber, 161–82. Grand Rapids: Zondervan, 2007.

Webber, Robert. *The Younger Evangelicals: Facing the Challenges of the New World*. Grand Rapids: Baker, 2002.

Wells, David. *No Place for Truth: Or, Whatever Happened to Evangelical Theology?* Grand Rapids: Eerdmans, 1994.

Westphal, Merold. *Overcoming Onto-Theology: Toward a Postmodern Christian Faith*. New York: Fordham University Press, 2001.

———. "A Reader's Guide to 'Reformed Epistemology.'" *Perspectives* 7.9 (1992) 10–13.

———. *Whose Community? Which Interpretation? Philosophical Hermeneutics for the Church*. Grand Rapids: Baker, 2009.

Wright, N. T. "How Can the Bible Be Authoritative?" *Vox Evangelica* 21 (1991) 7–32.

www.ingramcontent.com/pod-product-compliance
Lightning Source LLC
Chambersburg PA
CBHW030857170426
43193CB00009BA/642